MW00638382

Martha's Vineyard Outdoors

Martha's Vineyard Outdoors

Fishing, Hunting and Avoiding Divorce on a Small Island

to John:
the island made
me do it.
Nelson
Sigelman

NELSON SIGELMAN

Copyright 2017 Nelson Sigelman

Cover design by Glenn Wolff (glennwolff.com). All rights reserved. No part of this publication may be reproduced, distributed, or transmitted in any form or by any means, including photocopying, recording or other electronic or mechanical means without prior written permission of the publisher, except in the case of brief quotations embodied in critical reviews and certain other noncommercial uses permitted by copyright law.
All inquiries should be addressed to Nelson Sigelman, PO 4530, Vineyard Haven, MA 02568 or
www.marthasvineyardoutdoors.com.
ISBN-13: 9780692972304
ISBN-10: 0692972307

Photo Credits: Bluefish blitz photo courtesy Robert Schellhammer; Christin Carotta with bass, courtesy Bill Larsen; Nelson Sigelman with big striper, courtesy Leslie Look; Tisbury Pond Club, courtesy The Trustees archives and research center; photo of Albert Angelone courtesy Gerald R. Ford Library; trout photo courtesy of Tim Sheran. Bill Clinton and Vernon Jordan, Bob "Hawkeye" Jacobs and Stan Murphy by Ralph Stewart; Herbert Hancock by Betsy Corsiglia; dogs with decoys by Todd Cleland; and hunters at state forest by Ezra Newick are courtesy of the authors and The MV Times.

Painting of Roberto Germani courtesy Kib Bramhall. Marlan Sigelman, barrel of blue claws, turkeys in yard, Alabama photos, Bajan fisherman, lone fisherman at Cedar Tree Neck, Jimmy Klingensmith, Irene Henley and Olga Hirshhorn by author.

For Norma and Marlan,
the two big catches of my life.

Acknowledgments

THIS COLLECTION OF fishing and hunting columns arises out of the culture and traditions of Martha's Vineyard. I am grateful to many people who shared their stories with me over the years, and to my many hunting and fishing companions whom I have not attempted to name, fearing that I might leave one of them out.

All of these columns appeared first in The Martha's Vineyard Times. Publishing a newspaper is a team effort, and I am grateful for all the help and cooperation I received from the people I worked with over the course of my career. Thanks also to my longtime editor and friend, Doug Cabral, who gave me my start in journalism and whose wise counsel continues to guide me, and to Peter and Barbara Oberfest, the owners of The Times, for granting me the rights to my columns and the use of various photographs.

Several people were kind enough to read this collection and offer guidance, encouragement, and help along the way with all that is entailed in putting a book together. Thank you all.

My patient wife Norma and daughter Marlan have my love and gratitude.

And though he lies buried on the shore of an island salt pond where we once hunted together, in my dreams I still feel the muzzle of Tashmoo, my loyal Labrador retriever, who nuzzles me while I sleep.

Contents

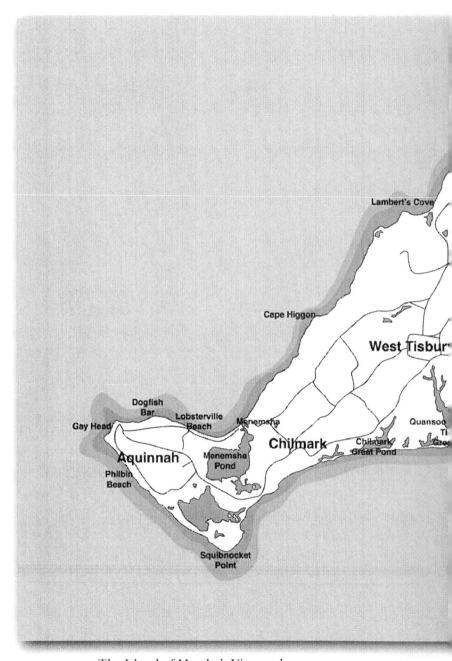

The Island of Martha's Vineyard

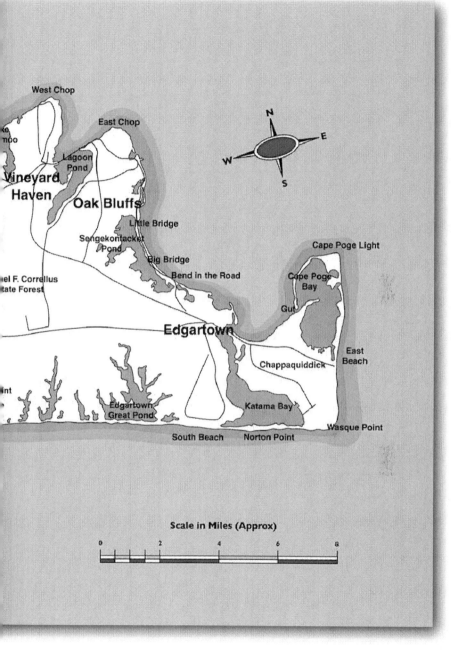

West Chop

East Chop

Lagoon
Pond

ke
moo

Vineyard
Haven

Oak Bluffs

Little Bridge

Sengekontacket
Pond

Big Bridge

el F. Correllus
tate Forest

Bend in the Road

Edgartown

int

Edgartown
Great Pond

Chappaquiddick

Katama Bay

South Beach

Norton Point

Cape Poge Light

Cape Poge
Bay

Gut

East
Beach

Wasque Point

N
W   E
S

Scale in Miles (Approx)

0   2   4   6   8

Introduction

AFTER TEN YEARS of driving from Boston to the Vineyard whenever I had an opportunity to go fishing, in the fall of 1989 I took a job at The Martha's Vineyard Times and moved into a winter rental in the port town of Vineyard Haven. I sold advertising for The Times, the newer of two competing weekly Island newspapers. I think I was pretty good at it, because I managed to sell myself to Norma Clinton.

I was lucky to meet Norma, a woman possessed of great patience and a deep understanding and appreciation for the hunting and fishing traditions that underpin upstate New York, where she grew up, and Martha's Vineyard, where she summered as a child and later lived and attended high school after her parents moved to the Island to live full-time. Our daughter Marlan was born in April 1991, and I was hooked. The Vineyard became my home.

A few years after I'd been working at The Times, editor and publisher Doug Cabral saw a kernel of talent in my writing and suggested I become a reporter. The first general news story I wrote concerned a house being built at Cape Poge on the remote, difficult to reach northeast corner of Chappaquiddick, a tiny, sometime island outpost that is part of Edgartown, at the eastern end of the Vineyard. The builder had hired a helicopter pilot to ferry gravel from a staging area at Bend-in-the-Road Beach to the building site, otherwise accessible by boat or over sand vehicle. I asked the pilot if I could go along.

I got into the helicopter, normally used for crop-dusting cranberry bogs in southeast Massachusetts, and the pilot, a character wearing a cowboy hat, told me not to touch or bump any of the levers in front of me. We were traveling over water carrying a sling with thousands of pounds of stone under us — and, oh yes, his Labrador retriever was sitting in the helicopter with us. But he was worried about me touching the controls? I sat frozen.

That story was my introduction to the fun, quirkiness, and what I would later realize is the vital and important nature of community journalism. As I gained more experience, I also recognized the challenges of a job that requires careful calibration when weighing individual privacy against the basic requirement of the job, which is to reveal what's important to the community. On more than one occasion I shook my head over the disturbing details in a police report and wrestled with how to tell the story. There was also pain. Reporting the untimely deaths of young people or the arrests of people I knew takes a toll.

The fun part was the range and breadth of stories and the people I got to know. I remember longtime Chilmark selectman, builder, and lobsterman Herbert Hancock and the battle to build a new Chilmark School — "These are little kids," Herbie said in response to state building code dictates on square footage. "Why do they need so much room?" Classic.

One day, as he lay dying at home, Herb called me up to say he had something for me. When I walked into his bedroom, he handed me his old Browning "humpback" shotgun, the gun he had used to take many deer, ducks and geese. It meant the world to me, and I have never shouldered the scuffed up stock of that twelve-gauge without thinking of Herbert and the rich island values he embodied.

Over the years, I met reporters from the large dailies on-island to cover a presidential visit. I was always struck by the contrast between their relationships with their readers — distant – with the newsmakers – closer. I always sat in one corner or another of The Times' large open office, and over the years readers (and lots of fishermen) walked right in to tell me about a story, ask a question, or vent angrily. Just the way it should be, I thought.

My first fishing column appeared in The MV Times in May 1990. It began: "First the rumors, then the fish. You start seeing a few trucks with rods on top and realize that maybe it is time to take care of all those things you kept talking about doing all winter: clean the reels, re-spool the line, tie some leaders, change the hooks … but there's no time now. The fish are here."

I had always liked to fish, but before moving to the Vineyard my hunting grounds had been only restaurants and supermarkets. My interest in deer hunting began after my good friend and hunting mentor Cooper "Coop" Gilkes, owner of Coop's Bait and Tackle in Edgartown, gave me a venison roast. Knowing I could not expect Coop to keep handing over prime cuts, I picked up a shotgun, and with expert guidance from several skilled Islanders, I learned to fill my own larder. Deer hunting has been an enriching experience on many levels.

My introduction to the joys of "waiting for a flight stupendous" and the Vineyard's rich waterfowling tradition began after Norma and I, and our young daughter Marlan, moved to Chilmark off Middle Road to begin a stint as caretakers on a 70-acre property owned by a New York architect. Thinking a dog would be good company for my family, and with no thought of ducks, I bought a headstrong black Labrador puppy from landscaper Steve Yaffe of Gay Head for $50 and named him Tashmoo.

More than a century ago, duck blinds were a common feature of the Island's ponds and bay. Though much diminished, duck hunting remains a popular Island activity. Once again, Coop had a role in the expansion of my outdoor pursuits. He invited me to go duck hunting on Chappaquiddick and bring Tashmoo along. That morning, responding to what every piece of his DNA told him to do, Tashmoo retrieved a duck from the icy waters of Cape Poge Bay on the eastern end of the Island. I was astounded. Years later I told people that my dog made me a duck hunter — I loved watching Tashmoo plunge into the water with unbridled enthusiasm, because that was what he knew he was born to do.

As my outdoor experiences broadened, my column portfolio expanded to include deer hunting and duck hunting, but mostly what I wrote about, whether fishing or hunting, was the character and characters of Martha's Vineyard. Over the years I covered significant news stories, but it was the fishing and hunting stories that island readers seemed to appreciate most, and for which I was known. The best compliments I received and the ones that meant the most, often relayed to me from Norma after someone had stopped her in the grocery store, came from people who prefaced their remarks by noting that he or she didn't fish or hunt but enjoyed what I had written in that particular week's column.

I enjoyed the freedom of writing a fishing column on an island where fishing is part of the shared culture. I used the column to have fun and also to advocate for things I care about, especially shore fishing access and conservation.

The Martha's Vineyard Striped Bass and Bluefish Derby figured large in my columns over the years, because this five-week fishing tournament held every fall is so central to Island life. Since the 1990s, roughly three thousand fishermen have registered annually for the derby, almost half of them Islanders. If you accept 17,000 as the year-round population and factor in fishermen who, by the third week of the derby, were late for dinner, never showed up for dinner, fell asleep at dinner, were late for work, went to work but weren't really there, developed double bagged eyes, and lost the ability to speak the English language, it is easy to see that the derby affects more Islanders than any other single event short of a winter power outage.

There have been funny derby stories, tragic stories, and wacky ones. I am fond of telling them to people I meet who are unfamiliar with the Vineyard, because I think they are so revealing of Island character and characters.

On occasion, I have been deep into the retelling of some derby tale and sensed that the person on the receiving end is not so interested in hearing about the time Hawkeye stripped down and jumped off Memorial Wharf in an effort to free an albacore snagged on the bottom of a ferry docked alongside, much to the horror and puzzlement of a female crew member.

And, I have been at cocktail parties where I described the return of legendary Dick Hathaway of Edgartown to the derby throne at age 70, and his fall from grace the following year, and noticed that the drama is lost on the innocent who probably intended to have a short, meaningless conversation as the shrimp got passed around.

Hunting is one of those topics fraught with political and cultural peril. Once, at a Chilmark dinner party, Norma rose from her seat, walked over to me, and put her hand over my mouth as I was just warming to a description of the finer aspects of shooting deer. I admit, I was laying it on a bit thick. Norma to the rescue.

The truth is that when I get talking about the derby or hunting, my enthusiasm for the topic often gets the better of me. Politics? Nah. The derby? Shooting ducks or geese? Roll out the anecdotes.

Often, during the usual party postmortem on the ride home, Norma will tell me that I talked too long about fishing and the derby.

"Couldn't you see that they weren't interested in fishing?" Norma asks.

"Yes," I say, "but I couldn't help myself."

And so it is with this collection of columns, which appear in chronological order.

Fishing

A bass and bluefish blitz at Wasque Rip.

"Father Neptune is no respecter of persons, and spatters his royal favors so lavishly and so impartially on the just and the unjust that, unless you are a believer in the 'longshore theory that 'salt water never hurts nobody,' and can take a thorough soaking philosophically and as a matter of course, you had better give up all thought of being a bass fisherman."

— FROM AN ESSAY PUBLISHED IN 1882 BY FISHERMAN AND WRITER FRANCIS ENDICOTT

Fishing by Canoe — Aloha Menemsha

(August 1990)

NORMA SAID, "HONEY, the canoe is a two-man canoe. It's a heavy canoe. It is not a one-man canoe."

I'd never seen the canoe but did I listen to her? Of course not. Unlike most new age sensitive guys I rarely listen to my girl friend when the subject is connected to fishing. "Hey, no problem," I told her.

Bonito were off Menemsha and I planned to add outriggers to the canoe "Islander" style, that is Vineyard/Tahitian in order to stay stable in the ocean chop. The canoe would allow me to reach the fish and avoid the mayhem of the jetties.

Edgartown Kahuna Paul Schultz gave me some old lobster pot buoys; I purchased a ten-foot PVC pole at those Kon Tiki outfitters, Ace Hardware; and Eddy Amaral of Oak Bluffs — think of Queequeg — provided some good advice based on his own experience. "Don't forget your lifejacket," Ed said.

Ed had rigged his canoe with floatation buoys made out of two-liter soda bottles attached to a pipe and was fly fishing for big blues in the middle of Cape Poge Pond. According to the story he reluctantly told me, Ed set the hook on a big bluefish, only to have the fish go one way and he the other.

The canoe was stored in the backyard of Norma's ex-husband, Glenn Andrews. A builder and craftsman, Glenn wasn't quite sure what I had in mind when I showed up to get the canoe but he found my whole idea of rigging it with an outrigger to go fly fishing for bonito intriguing.

Glenn was not a fisherman so my excited mutterings about bonito were lost on him, but he willingly joined in and helped me pound a white foam lobster buoy on to each end of the PVC pole — his craftsmanship evident because while I used a rock, he went to the trouble of getting a hammer. Glenn helped me lift the heavy fiberglass canoe on top of my Isuzu trooper.

"Well, Glenn, what do you think?" I asked, anxious to get fishing. "I think the bonito are in trouble," he answered. He was only 50 percent correct.

Lobsterville Beach was quiet when I arrived. Fishermen lined the Menemsha and Lobsterville jetties, some casting fly rods, others spinning rods. At the end of each jetty, they were clustered like mountain goats on the edge of a precipice. Fishermen in small boats and canoes floated a respectful distance from each jetty.

Suddenly, bonito began breaking the surface of the water in a feeding frenzy. Fishermen responded the same way. Lures criss-crossed and one man was just about strangled in another man's fishing line. Hooking a bonito was the easy part; getting off the jetty without any lures embedded in you was the challenge. Well, I don't have to deal with this, I thought, I have a canoe.

Without anyone around to assist me the canoe proved to be heavier to lift off the vehicle roof than I had anticipated so I let it drop off with a crash. Not elegant but it was off. Quickly, I loaded a fly rod, net, oar, and half a cinder block tied to a rope for use as an anchor. I lashed down the PVC-lobster-buoy-outrigger and was ready to go — about ten feet!

The fish began to break. I watched a fly fisherman as his rod arched over under the weight of a fish. I strained to pull the canoe and traveled five more feet in the soft beach sand. I felt like a horse at the Ag Fair draft horse competition and knew it would not be easy to reach the beach.

"You need some help?" asked a man standing with his son as they looked at me sympathetically while I lay gasping for breath in the sand. With their assistance I made it to the water's edge and contemplated my situation. The wind appeared to be blowing about 25 knots out of the southwest, and the water had a nice chop. Roberto, Brian and Marco sat out in their one-man canoes fly fishing at anchor.

I recognized that the wind was quite strong, my canoe was quite long, and the other fly fishermen were fishing in smaller, lighter canoes and knew what they were doing. The fish broke again. Without hesitation I jumped into the back of the canoe (experienced canoeists know this was my second mistake) and pushed off from the beach at a furious paddle.

The canoe sliced through the water as the wind drove me forward. In a moment I was up to the other canoeists. In two moments I was past them. I tried to turn the canoe but because I was seated in the stern, rather than in the middle, I could not turn the bow into the wind and my furious paddling only propelled me faster in a direction I did not want to go. The other canoeists stopped casting and eyed me curiously. I managed a weak smile.

Now off the jetties, I still paddled as fishermen standing on the rocks watched me with a combination of amusement and concern. I straightened up and did my best, despite my desperate paddling and even more desperate embarrassment, to maintain an attitude of nonchalance that proclaimed: "Hey, I wanted to get sucked into the channel."

For good measure bonito started to break behind me. But I was full in the current and could only manage a momentary glance as I was vacuumed into Menemsha Pond by the tidal flow. I paddled furiously to reach the shore on the Lobsterville side of the channel and spare myself from having to hitch-hike from Menemsha back to the beach. Exhausted, I made it ashore and with some help from Robert Heaphy got the canoe back on my vehicle.

"Honey," Norma said, after I'd arrived home and recounted my story. "I told you the canoe is a two-man canoe. It's a heavy canoe. It's not a one-man canoe."

In this 1990 Christmas card, Nelson and Norma
anticipate the birth of Marlan in March.

It's a Bird! It's a Plane! It's a WHAT?

This charter fishing trip brought some unexpected thrills.
(August 1990)

EDGARTOWN CAPTAIN CHARLIE Blair knows all about the mako shark's reputation for being a tough fighter but I doubt he ever expected to go toe to toe with one in a ring measuring eight by ten feet. The ring I'm referring to was the deck of the Nisa, Charlie's 33-foot charter boat, not exactly the kind of place you want to slug it out with a very angry 200-pound mako shark. In fact, you might be better off up against Mike Tyson — at least you could swim for it!

The corner man for this bout was first mate Elizabeth Staples. The fishermen on board were Matt Weiner, 19, and his brother Dave, 16, from Westchester and Chilmark, and their friends, Jeff White, 19, and Andy George, 13. For the past eight years Dave and Matt's dad had arranged for the boys to fish with Captain Blair, usually for bluefish. This summer Matt asked if they could try shark fishing.

Andy was the first one to see a fin cutting through the water heading for the bait floating on a line some distance behind the boat. Charlie immediately yelled down from the bridge that it was a mako and for Jeff, who was wearing the stand-up harness that would be used to support the fishing rod he was holding, to get ready for some action.

It didn't take long. The mako took the bait about 100 feet out. Jeff set the hook with a sharp tug and the fish jumped about 10 feet in the air. That was just the warmup though, because the next thing the fishermen knew the mako was heading straight for the boat trying to set a new record in the mako 100-foot dash.

Estimates vary regarding the height of the next jump. Elizabeth said it was higher than the bridge of the boat — all she saw when she looked up was the white belly of the shark. Dave figured it was at least 15 feet in the air, but nobody stood waiting to hang any gold medals around the mako's thick neck because the fish was directly over the boat.

"We had enough time to look up," Jeff said. "You could tell he was coming in the boat; he was over our heads — way over our heads. Charlie jumped back and grabbed me. I just dropped the rod and the mako hit the stern and bounced in."

Not surprisingly, everybody acted like, well, like a 200-pound very angry mako had just jumped onto the deck of the boat. Elizabeth dropped the chum bucket from which she'd been ladling pieces of bait over the side to attract sharks, and headed for the bow. Andy headed for the cabin and Dave joined his brother up on the bridge in about two seconds. Elizabeth said it was a good thing the kids were young and agile, although I know that some older fishermen would get agile real quick faced with an incoming mako.

The mako was now on the deck thrashing and flailing away, gear and ropes flying everywhere. Charlie yelled for Elizabeth to hand him the harpoon and he struck the mako as it jumped around on the deck. The mako's wild flailing around on the deck entangled it in the lines, which allowed Charlie and Elizabeth an opportunity to tie off the fish and hang it over the side.

Charlie said it was all pretty scary and he was just happy everybody was safe. Mr. Weiner said next year the kids will go fishing for blues.

You know, I'm not very good at remembering the names of movies, but wasn't there a story about a shark and some island …

Hooking Up Despite Life's Snags

A Colorado fisherman fulfills his goal to catch a bonito on the fly rod.
(July 1992)

FANCY FLY FISHING catalogs are filled with almost everything a would be fisherman might want for fishing shore or stream: strong, flexible rods incorporating the latest in technology; precision crafted fly reels costing hundreds of dollars; clothing to satisfy the most fashion conscious angler; and enough little doodads to hang off every clip and stuff in every pocket of the largest fly vest.

But there are no wheelchairs in fly fishing catalogs. Cliff Thompson, who visited the Island last week to do a little bonito fishing, would be the first to tell you that fishing from a wheelchair isn't easy. Yet, it's said with a matter-of-fact tone, that puts the statement in the category of other fishermen's complaints that include tangles, knots, and poor casts. A man with the attitude and determination that Cliff Thompson demonstrates is not about to let a wheelchair ever get in the way of some good fishing, even if the wheel hub occasionally snags his line.

More than 10 years ago, living in the small town of Beaver Creek, Colo., Cliff went over the handlebars of a bicycle in what he terms, "a goofy accident." At the emergency room in Denver, the orthopedic surgeon, Lonnie Chipman, told Cliff, "son, you better give up any hope of walking again," and Cliff replied, "Thanks doc, I kind of figured that out."

Cliff said he'd known immediately what had happened, describing it as a feeling similar to when you hit your funny bone, "only" he said, "in this case it lasts forever."

Not long after his accident, Cliff started a small community newspaper. While making a sales call, he met Carey Marcus, the owner of a small clothing store and a dedicated fresh water fly fisherman. He was tying up some flies, and when Cliff expressed surprise that any fish would hit something so small, Carey told him he should see for himself. Cliff had never thought of fly fishing but he was willing to try anything once, and together they headed for a lake outside of town. Carey caught a bunch of fish, and Cliff just flogged the water. But despite his initial lack of success, Cliff fell in love with fly fishing.

Boats and rafts helped him overcome the limits of wheelchair access. Cliff laughs as he states, "The stories of me going in the water are legion." Interestingly enough, the person who first introduced Cliff to saltwater fly fishing was Lonnie Chipman, the doctor he'd met in the emergency room.

Dr. Chipman and his wife, both avid fly fishermen, had moved near Beaver Creek, and when they found out that Cliff had taken up fly fishing, they started inviting him along on various fishing trips. Bonefish in the Bahamas were a whole different experience from fresh water, and Cliff started turning his attention to the ocean.

Summer visits to the home of his parents on Cape Cod also gave him the opportunity to rig up their small Boston Whaler boat with a platform he could lash his chair to and chase blues whenever he could find someone to operate it.

While in Colorado this winter, he kept hearing about bonito from his friend, Danny, who works at the Wood's Hole Biological Laboratory in Falmouth. He described their slashing speed through the water chasing bait, and Cliff figured if he was already going to be on the Cape fishing for blues, he ought to try going after bonito too. So he wrote a letter to Lou Tabory, a well-known fly fisherman and author who wrote back that there was only one place to go: Martha's Vineyard.

Last Thursday, Cliff got to visit the Island, rolling off the Steamship Authority ferry, fly rod in hand, ready for a chance at getting his first bonito with "Bonito" Eddy Lepore. With a nickname like that, he felt in good hands as they headed out in Eddy's small tin boat for the waters around the Oak Bluffs Steamship Authority dock, home to a large school of baitfish and marauding pods of bonito.

Eddy had tied up some small white deceivers flies, and it wasn't long after the tide started to run that the bonito started bursting through rushing schools of baitfish. Cliff was just bringing his fly back when he felt the strike. The fly line zipped through the water producing an immediate ear to ear grin as the bonito lived up to all its advance billing.

Fishing is a sport that can put us in touch with our natural environment and give us all an appreciation for the world around us. Sometimes, the same may be said of the fishermen we meet.

It Takes a Big Gaff to Land a Bucket

An offshore trip provided an opportunity for some mischief. (August 1993)

VENTURING OFFSHORE TO go fishing can be an exciting and beautiful experience with the opportunity for a real adventure. You just never know what you're going to catch, particularly when you start to doze off.

Dale McClure of Vineyard Haven had gotten a new boat and wanted to go out and do a little tuna fishing. So he invited his friends, David Steere of West Tisbury and Cooper Gilkes of Edgartown, to go along. Coop had just gotten in from the Oak Bluffs shark tournament, but with the lure of tuna and blue water it didn't take much to motivate him. So the three fishermen met in Menemsha and headed offshore at four in the morning.

This was David's first trip offshore tuna fishing and he had a lot of questions for Coop, who had rigged all the rods with the same lure except one, telling David with the certainty of experience, "That's the one they'll hit every time." But despite Coop's appetizer and main course trolling arrangement, they couldn't raise a fish.

They trolled and they trolled, almost out to the shipping lanes. For four and one half hours they trolled, on an ocean so flat and calm that you couldn't help but fall asleep. And that's exactly what David did. He went back to a chair that was between the rods and fell fast asleep.

Now, Coop is a fisherman who knows how to take advantage of every opportunity, and that includes putting one over on his fishing companions. So, recognizing a chance to have some fun, he turned to Dale, motioned to the sleeping David, and whispered, "The bucket."

"So I sneak out very quietly," Cooper says with a laugh, "and, of course, I picked the rod that I said was gonna get hit, right, and I pulled the line in by hand. I didn't reel it in, I pulled it in, took the lure off, took the clip, put it on a five gallon brown bucket, reached over the side and dropped it in the water. Then I headed for the wheelhouse. Well, in my haste headin' for the wheelhouse I got the damn line around my ankle. All of a sudden, as I go through the wheelhouse door I'm findin' myself attached to a five gallon bucket goin' ninety miles an hour due south!"

As Coop worked to free himself, the line went tight, driving the bucket very deep. Meanwhile, David was still sleeping through all of it, presumably dreaming of the big one. And that's what he thought he'd hooked, because when Coop finally got clear of the line and let it go, it sounded, Coop says, "like the biggest tuna hit you ever saw in your life! Zzzzzz...," the line was screaming and that woke David right up out of his chair.

"So David woke right up," Coop says, "and you could see him trying to get himself together, and we're laughing in the wheelhouse. So he goes, 'What do I do? What do I do?' So I walk back, cool as a cucumber, right, tryin' to keep a straight face, and David goes, 'It hit that rod, you were right. I don't believe it.'

"So he tries to get the rod out of the rod holder, but the rod is buckling and he can't get it out. I mean Dale is putting the coals to it [the boat throttle] pretty good, right, and this bucket now is 250 yards back. So he can't get the rod out and I tell him to relax the drag just a little bit, and lines going out, and we get him in a harness, all rigged up."

Now two momentous battles ensue – one between David and his bucket; the other by Cooper and Dale to keep from laughing. Finally, after fifteen minutes the bucket just breaks the surface of the water about 25 yards back and David turns to Cooper, asking, "What color is that thing?" To which Coop replies with a straight face and the hint of a big fish, "Jeez, looks brown to me, David."

David gets the bucket in even closer and now Coop says, "Dale comes out and he brings a little bluefish gaff with him. David looks up, and I swear, if I'd had a video camera I'd a made a million bucks. David looks up, sweat's pouring off him, and he looks at Dale and says, 'No! No! No! Get the big gaff. Get the big gaff. I don't wanna lose him!'"

In moments of excitement or stress we all say things we sometimes regret. It is safe to say that David will forever regret telling Dale to "get the big gaff" as long as fishing stories are told to entertain around Island fireplaces in winter.

And, by the way, David landed his bucket.

Fisherman's Theory of Distant Relativity

President Clinton's return visit to the Island prompts a concern. (August 1994)

My wife Norma's maiden name is Clinton. I mention this to highlight one of the undeniable liabilities of a year round Vineyard address: the summer visit by distant relatives. And when you fish that invariably means you have to end up taking them fishing.

Now, I don't know if Bill will want to go out this year, but if he does I sure hope I don't go through what I went through with my Uncle Fred. See, last year my Uncle Fred and Aunt Ruthy, who live in Virginia, decided that the third weekend in August would be a great time to visit the Island of Martha's Vineyard. Of course Bill also was visiting but figuring that Fred and Ruthy were only going to be here for the weekend I never bothered to hook up with Bill, which set the stage for the "relative visit from Hell."

Fred is one of those guys who spent one half of his life working for the government and the other half complaining about the government, and now that he's retired he's expanded his complaining to include a wider variety of things. During his visit, that included the muffins at the bed and breakfast owned by our friends (A little tip here: never arrange for relatives to stay anywhere people know you.), and the constant observation that the prices are high and the Island is crowded the third weekend in August. This observation was repeated endlessly on a Friday evening as we searched for a restaurant without a wait. Which brings me to our fishing trip.

As every good fisherman knows, the key to success is preparation and that includes your fishing tackle. That's why I have two sets of gear, the rods that I use and the stuff I let other people use. And believe me, the first time you let some cousin borrow your custom nine foot surf rod and then go to use it the next time only to have it sound like a gravel mixer when you go to turn the handle you'll understand the need for a relative rod.

So on a Saturday afternoon I put my boat in the water at the Vineyard Haven lagoon launch area and headed to a spot off of Eel Pond in Edgartown where I'd caught some small blues. As I got the boat ready it began.

"You know," Fred started in the way of making fishing conversation, "when we lived in Hawaii I used to go fishing for kava kava. Do you know what those are?"

"No," I answered trying to show even minimal interest in a fishing story from Fred's Hawaii years.

"Oh, those kava kava are a great fish. We'd take a boat out and go after them. Good eating, too."

This was all well and good as far as it went but the problem was that apparently Hawaii was the only place Fred had ever gone fishing and kava kava was the only fish he'd ever caught. I know this because ten minutes out of the Lagoon I heard the kava kava story again. And again, and again. Which reduced me to the very effective technique of starting the engine and moving every time the kava kava story started.

"So, Nelson, like I was saying when I was in ..." vrooooommm.

Off Eel Pond we found the small school of blues and Fred had a grand old time hooking a couple of them which I dutifully netted. Of course it was nothing like the time he went fishing in Hawaii but it sure beat wandering up and down Main Street on a hot Saturday afternoon comparing prices to those back home and then expounding on the fact to everyone within tourist T-shirt range. On the way back the wind picked up and we had a wet ride back but the sound of the engine and Fred's hunkered down posture lent a sort of peacefulness to the whole scene as we rounded East Chop.

Fred enjoyed our little trip almost as much as the fondly remembered kava kava fishing, while I was left with only one question: "What the hell is a goddamn kava kava?"

A few days later my mother, who was also down visiting, and Fred and Ruthy went to catch the noon ferry from Vineyard Haven. Only there was one small glitch. My mother had assumed that her reservation was for Wednesday and it had in fact been for Tuesday. So Fred and Ruthy got to experience the fondest of Vineyard summer attractions, the standby line.

During the seven hours that they waited, with neither Fred nor Ruthy speaking to my mother, Fred used this opportunity to ingratiate himself with the Steamship Authority employees by offering his opinion on how the entire operation could be better run. Needless to say, everyone working in the crowded Steamship lot in the 90 degree summer heat of that day was very interested in all of Fred's suggestions and Fred was at a loss to understand their "attitude."

So, Bill, I know you're family and I'll do my best if you'd like to do some fishing this trip. Please, just don't tell me any stories about kava kava.

Reel Presidents Don't
Look for Birdies

President Jimmy Carter was no duffer in waders.
(September 1994)

T HE PRESIDENTIAL VACATION is over, and it was obvious during Bill
Clinton's ten day stay that golf is his favorite activity. You'd
think an Arkansas boy would have just a touch of bass fishing in
his blood.

Not that I have anything against golf, but the game doesn't
strike me as a release; people play golf and still manage to talk
about business and politics. In the end, golf is simply one long conversation broken up by intermittent efforts to put a small white ball
in a hole marked by a flag. Ask a group of golfers what they talked
about during their 18 holes and they'll mention any number of
things, little of it golf related.

Fishing is different. Fishermen talk about fishing if they have
any conversation at all. In that sense the sport of fishing serves a
president very well. Presidents golf with people described as "power
brokers," they fish with people described as fishermen. Fresh or
saltwater, it is a sport that allows for introspection and provides a
connection to the environment: the surf and salt air or a stream
and the cool forest smell.

But more importantly fishing allows us to have a conversation with ourselves and when you are the president, and at the center of as many conversations as time and scheduling allows, that may be the biggest benefit of all. The American people find something reassuring about a president standing with fishing rod in hand.

President Bill Clinton and Washington lawyer Vernon Jordan share a golf cart at Farm Neck Golf Club in Oak Bluffs.

Imagine two photos. One shows the president on the golf course cupping his hand and whispering to a fellow golfer in his party with a smile on his face; the other shows the same two people in waders holding rods by the beach. The first photo evokes the feeling of politicking and deal making, the second, a humorous story. Fishing has to be good for a few percentage points in the polls.

I talked fishing and presidents the other day with Howell Raines, editorial page editor for the New York Times and a southerner with a love of fishing described so well in his book, "Fly Fishing Through The Midlife Crisis."

Asked to name the best presidential fishermen, Mr. Raines allowed that it's always difficult to compare people from different eras, but his choice for the best all around 20th century fly fisherman would be Jimmy Carter. For the level of expertise, the variety of fish caught, and general fly tying skill, Carter, he said, was the best. Yet, he added, Hoover was also a skilled fisherman, leading to the conclusion that Carter was the best Democratic fisherman and Hoover the best Republican.

"Eisenhower," he said, "loved to fish," but was not particularly an artful trout fisherman and "tended to break fish off at the strike." Bush, he remarked, is a good fisherman, but primarily a bait caster.

I hesitated to make too much of this, yet as we spoke I could not help thinking that of all our retired presidents the activities of former President Carter command the most respect as he is busy constructing homes for the poor and pursuing efforts to foster world peace. I contrasted this with Reagan, who cashed in his prestige with the Japanese for a $2 million speech, and Gerald Ford, a golfer, who seems to have used his stint as president as a path to better greens. Did fishing make a difference?

Certainly fishing, Mr. Raines said, is a sport from which different people draw different rewards: "Hoover liked the solitude of fishing and wrote in his book that `other than when he's praying, the only time that a president can be alone with his thoughts is when he's fishing.' He also liked the fact that in his day there were no newspaper people around.

"Now, Carter responded more to the challenge. He talked about the fact that the trout doesn't care if you're a sixteen-year-old farm boy or president of the United States.

"It treats you the same. And he liked the intricacies of picking the right fly, reading the current and getting the right float over the fish. I guess in the end it comes to the same thing, if you have a job that is totally consuming, as the presidency must be, you need the ability to find something that will absorb you and take you away from that. I think also the importance of place has a lot to do with it. Hoover liked Camp Rapidan, which is a beautiful spot up in the Blue Ridge, it's cool and shaded and the opposite of what the White House was like even in his day. Carter used to go to Camp David and secretly take a helicopter to fish Spring Creek near Penn State."

The idea of even a president sneaking out to his favorite fishing hole is appealing and something to which every fisherman can relate. In the end, maybe Howell Raines is correct when he says that everyone needs an escape. It just seems that of all the choices open to a president on Martha's Vineyard, fishing is a pretty good one. Maybe next year Bill.

A Bass — Not Far From the Madding Crowd

Casting to the rhythm of the Godfather of Soul feels right.
(August 1994)

Owwww! PAPA'S GOT a brand new bag. Uh!
I don't usually fish to the background sounds of James Brown, the Godfather of Soul, but sometimes I just don't feel like getting back in the car and moving.

It was kind of late and I was pretty tired, but it was too beautiful a night not to get out for a few hours of tossing a line. A slight cold front had come in, a welcome early touch of fall, and the lethargy of 90 percent humidity was replaced with the anticipation of autumn's first strike. So I'd left the house around 9 p.m. and headed up to Menemsha to look for some stripers along the beach. This is a nice place to fish, with easy parking and a short walk; just perfect when your body says "bed," but your spirit says "fish."

I pulled into the parking lot, expecting to see the usual assortment of boaters, strollers, jetty fishermen, and sunset lingerers, and hoped to hear the sounds of breaking bass (rhymes with mass) along the beach. Instead, the only sound coming from the beach was that of a throbbing bass (rhymes with vase) accompanied by the high-pitched cry of "Eeeewwww ... Get on up ... Come on now

... Get on up", punctuated by the exhortations of the DJ to "get dancin'."

I thought of getting back in the car and driving to Squibnocket or Lobsterville, but I had allotted just enough energy for a trip to one spot. Well, I thought to myself, I'm here and maybe it won't be so loud up the beach. And it's not that I'm against parties, I just like to do my fishing surrounded by the sounds that God intended without the need of a portable generator.

I got out of the car and started to put on my waders when one of the revelers approached; after all, everyone loves to talk to a fisherman.

"Hey, man," he said, walking over as I tightened my wader belt, "you gonna go fishing?"

That answer seemed rather obvious, but in the spirit of the summer of 1994, I decided to give him the benefit of the doubt and answered that, yes, I indeed had put on waders and a fishing vest because I was going fishing.

This raised his level of enthusiasm and, sensing a kindred spirit, he offered that he, too, enjoyed fishing. Then, as if sharing a precious bit of news, he pointed to the area just past where the sailboats moor off the beach and said, "Wow, man, look at that slick out there. I wish I had my rod with me, but I left it at home."

I turned in the direction of his "slick" which, if it had been a fish slick, would have been truly impressive and signaled the presence of a school of about one million fish off Menemsha Beach. But unfortunately it was no more than the sheen of the ocean at night. I started to walk down the beach and he called after me, "If you get any extra bluefish you don't want, just leave them on the hood of my truck, the black one over there. Good luck."

I made my way past the dancing, cheering, partying crowd and shielded my eyes from the glare of portable lights until I reached the welcome darkness of the beach. Carefully, I searched the surface of the water for the slightest ripple of activity that would reveal the presence of a feeding striped bass, as I trudged slowly through the sand towards the first outcropping of boulders where the beach ends. The sounds of the party continued to play over the beach, driving on the wind, but lingered in the background as the channel gong echoed in the darkness, a welcome metronome of the sea. The gravel along the shoreline rustled in the wash of the waves and I remembered why I had roused myself from the comfort of my couch, as a bright half-moon rose above the hills behind me, casting muted shadows on the beach.

I started to cast to areas that I thought might hold fish, working in an arc from left to right, searching the swirls and eddies around the rocks for a lazy summer striper lying in wait in the current for an easy sand eel snack. The time slowly passed and my casting settled into a rhythm of its own, unhurried and unconcerned.

Suddenly, the slow retrieve of my fly was interrupted by a watery explosion that sent salt spray shimmering under the moonlight in all directions, as a small striper left the water and catapulted over itself. For a moment, I was taken by surprise at this very unstriper like show of fishing gymnastics, and wondered what I'd hooked, until the steady pull on my line told me that I had a striper. Careful to avoid the rocks, I held the rod tip high and slowly played the bass to the beach until it lay in the sand.

And you will never truly see the full beauty of a striped bass until you have had the opportunity to view it's black-greenish stripes glistening in the moonlight on a beach, for this is truly the easel that was meant to frame a bass.

Carefully, I removed the hook from its jaw and held the fish in the water until, with one kick of its tail, it swam off to the current and eddies of the rocks. Then I walked back up the beach and went home.

Jamie Had a Shadow

This friendship just needed time to grow.
(June 1995)

F ISHING SUCCESS ATTRACTS attention, sometimes unwelcome by the fisherman who, through dint of effort and skill, has earned a reputation for finding fish when others can not. It is one thing to be among the crowd at Wasque rip, a prime fishing spot on the southeast corner of the Vineyard, and have someone copy your choice of plug. Imitation, as they say, is the sincerest form of flattery. It is quite another to be followed, to fish with a shadow.

And Jamie had a shadow.

Not a bad guy. Bob was well-meaning and nice enough. It's just that he was like a big double-wad of bubble gum on the bottom of Jamie's waders. And no matter how Jamie tried to scrape him off, Bob just kept sticking around.

Jamie first noticed it one morning at Wasque. The blues were slamming plugs in the rip and a line of fishermen were hooked up. As usual, fishing excitement started to give way to fishing mayhem with tangled lines and snapping fish on the beach. Jamie, a fly fisherman, decided to leave the crowd and fish a stretch of beach not far away between the rock pile and Cape Poge lighthouse on the northeast corner of Chappaquiddick.

Jamie had no sooner made his first cast than down the beach he saw Bob coming his way. And Jamie hooked a fish. Pavlov's theory is as true for fishermen as it was for hungry dogs. Jamie regretted the hook-up the minute he felt his line go taut. Bob, seeing Jamie had found fish, pulled right up behind Jamie's truck in a manner that would do the Steamship Authority vehicle loaders proud and began to fish beside him.

Wherever Jamie fished it seemed Bob would turn up. He was Jamie's self-designated best friend and no matter how Jamie tried to get it across that the feeling was not mutual he could not get that gum off his shoe. Bob just stuck around. The worm hatch at Tashmoo finally provided Jamie with a way to make his point.

Every spring a species of small mud worms swarm in selected coastal bays and ponds of New England. About an inch and a half long, they zigzag just below the surface of the water, sometimes rising to the surface, looking for what one assumes is worm love. However, love is not without risks, even when you are a worm, and all this activity attracts the attention of feeding striped bass.

Like politicians around a tray of cocktail shrimp, stripers cannot resist a worm hatch buffet. Even in the late afternoon, stripers will "sip" worms from the surface of the water. During particularly active hatches on calm days, the surface of Tashmoo is dotted with rippling circles expanding from the spot where a worm disappeared like a striper canapé.

The first evening Jamie fished the hatch, Bob showed up right beside him. Jamie's patience was finally at an end. In no uncertain terms he let Bob know he didn't appreciate his company. But Bob just didn't seem to get it. After about fifteen minutes of a frosty silence he started talking to Jamie again as though nothing had happened. Bob was a human with the personality of a Labrador retriever.

"Hey, Jamie what do you think about a green sand eel? You think I should try that?" he asked.

"Hey, do whatever you want, Bob," Jamie replied.

"What do you think, slow or fast retrieve?"

"I don't care."

"You're doin' fast though, huh?"

And so the conversation went.

Jamie had been fishing off a small point where the water got progressively deeper and dropped off at a small ledge. It gave him an idea.

The next evening he went out earlier than normal to Tashmoo with a milk crate with a few bricks attached for weight. The tide was low and rising. Jamie waded out to the ledge, stood on his milk crate and started fishing. Sure enough, along came Bob.

Bob immediately started wading out to take his usual position next to Jamie who appeared to only be standing in water up to his waist. Bob stepped off the ledge. Down he went into the water flailing and splashing away. Jamie thought it was funny at first until he realized Bob was having trouble making it back to shore.

Jamie hopped off the crate and made his way to Bob and reached out to pull him back to the shallows. Both fishermen got back to shore and emptied their waders of water. Bob had lost his fly rod when he started flailing his arms in the deep water.

"Thanks a lot Jamie, I really appreciate it," Bob said with an expression of sincerity that made Jamie feel worse than he already did.

"Hey Bob," Jamie told him, "c'mon with me, I've got another fly rod in my truck. Why don't we go check out Sengekontacket?"

"Sounds great to me."

Sometimes friendships start in the strangest ways.

Rock 'n' Roll 'n' Troll: All Systems A-Okay

A tuna fisherman returns to Earth.
(August 1995)

MY FIRST OFFSHORE tuna fishing trip has given me much in common with the astronauts depicted in the hit movie "Apollo 13." That film details the astronauts harrowing trip to the moon and their return to earth.

During the summer months, many Island fishermen with adequate boats (and some without) travel south of the Vineyard to the offshore waters where the deep blue color of the sea heralds an entry into another world. It is a place where yellowfin and bluefin tuna, dolphin (mahi-mahi), mako and blue sharks, and other open ocean gamesters can strike at any time. Whales breach, white marlin slash bait on the surface, and few fishermen returning from an offshore fishing trip fail to become caught up in the excitement and beauty, or look forward to their next opportunity to venture south.

I had never been offshore, other than the time I worked my way from Japan to the States on board a Norwegian oil tanker — hardly a trolling platform. So, when Cooper Gilkes called me at the The Times last Friday to invite me along on a tuna trip the next day with Dale McClure and David Steere, it seemed like the perfect opportunity to see what offshore fishing was all about. Particularly since the weather had been still and windless all week. I was to meet them at 4 a.m., Saturday in Menemsha Harbor.

I called my wife Norma, a woman possessed of a great deal of Island common sense, to let her know about the invitation. I told her I would be fishing with Cooper, Dale McClure, and David Steere. Norma began to laugh.

"Honey, those three guys are going to have you for lunch. That's why they're taking you. Have you seen the size of Dale McClure? It'll be like the Green Giant pickin' pea pods," she giggled, suggesting that my buddy Coop and his friends might enjoy having some fun at my expense.

But if you're going to dish it out, I thought, you've got to be willing to take it. The alarm was set, I closed my eyes for what seemed a moment, and I was standing at the dock half asleep when Dale eased his 35-foot Duffy, the Marion M., next to the Menemsha gas dock as neatly as could be.

Coop pulled up and we loaded the offshore rods into the boat. Pick up one of these fishing tools and you know serious fish are on the agenda. Fishing reels the size of a big coffee can and holding up to 700 yards of line, depending on the reel, sit on short stout rods meant to lift hundreds of pounds from the ocean's depths. Of course, the lifting of any piscatorial heavyweight requires that all that heavy, strong fishing gear be coupled to an equally strong back and tireless arm capable of cranking endlessly away.

Menemsha was surprisingly quiet for an early Saturday morning with few boats gearing up to head out offshore. The wind had also stiffened considerably from the lazy breezes of the entire week. The weather report called for increasing winds to 30 knots and a small craft advisory. Coop commented it would be "chunky" on our way back that afternoon. I dwelled on the real meaning of chunky in silence as Dale pushed the throttle down and the boat parted the swells already beginning to rise before the wind as we headed south past Gay Head light, which marks the western end of the Island.

David went below to nap. I peered into the fading gray of night reflected in the waves as we passed Nomans island, a small unoccupied piece of land south of the Vineyard and the last piece of dry earth we would see until we returned.

I had imagined a sun-drenched day on a blue mirrored ocean interrupted only by the shout of "Fish on!" Instead, I was an olive in an ocean cocktail mixer as the wind and ocean continued to rise. Dale decided it was time to get David out of bed. Coop laughed in agreement and the throttle was pushed forward. Unable to sleep as a human ping pong ball, David soon appeared from the cabin.

I am convinced it is no accident many of the best seamen throughout history have been men of bulk and size. A great deal of gravitational mass is necessary to keep one's feet firmly on deck while the horizon gyrates in front of your eyes. Dale, a big bearded man who looks every bit the sea captain, sat with his hands on the wheel firmly planted in a high stool that, though unbolted to the deck, rarely moved. Coop nimbly walked down the ever tilting deck to the stern and let out the lures. David, compact and solid, gave him a hand. I simply tried to focus the eyeballs rattling around in my head.

We began to troll; and troll; and troll. Unbroken monotony interrupted only by the heaving waves and tunes of Dale's favorite country-western music. We hadn't even caught a fish yet and I was exhausted from the effort required to stay upright and clench my stomach. I had never been seasick in my life but started to feel queasy.

One of the first points of boating etiquette Dale had mentioned was, "If you're gonna get sick do it over the side." I made my way out of the wheelhouse and stood on the deck, poised to vomit. Did I mention that Coop had brought his video camera?

I summoned up my will power tempered in the fencing halls of Japan and told myself that unless I wanted to become a feature film clip on the television at Coop's tackle shop I was not going to get sick. Sheer will overcame absolute nausea. I made my way back into the wheelhouse and slumped in a chair propped in the corner.

We continued to troll through 8- to 10-foot seas without so much as a bluefish. Dale mentioned matter-of-factly, "Those are some pretty big piles of water going by us." The radio crackled and another fishing boat commented, "It's like a roller coaster out here." I remembered that I would never go on the roller coaster at any amusement park. But now I was on it and couldn't get off. I wedged myself into a corner and surprisingly began to doze.

When I opened my eyes I watched the most amazing act of the entire morning. While David ate potato chips and took the wheel, Dale went into the cabin and cooked us all egg and bologna sandwiches. One trip into the cabin and I would have been a goner, and there was Dale cooking. Up from the hatchway he came and handed me a sandwich. I may have been hungry, I really had no way of telling.

"Thanks a lot, Dale," I said, "but to tell you the truth I haven't the slightest idea where my stomach is located." David, Dale, and Coop seemed to have no problem locating theirs. They ate their sandwiches and mine.

I continued to doze and they continued to troll. Then in my muddled consciousness I heard Coop mention getting the lures in before Nomans. I stood up and looked out. There was Nomans. Soon, we were rounding Gay Head.

I may not have traveled to the moon and back but I had certainly experienced weightlessness, and I doubt any returning astronaut was any happier than I was when I saw the entrance to Menemsha Harbor.

Another Typical Bonito Season
No Matter How Saturn Moves

A fisherman turns to La Toya Jackson for an answer to the bonito season.
(July 1996)

I AM READY FOR bonito. Those small football shaped mini-tuna that slice, rather than swim through the water. They are the perfect antidote to the mid-summer fishing doldrums when striped bass become scarce.

Schools of bonito usually begin to appear in Island waters by the end of July. The Oak Bluffs steamship wharf is often their first stop, but Menemsha is just as likely to attract the first arrivals. Fishermen spend a great deal of time speculating and theorizing about fishing. Predicting the abundance or lack of bonito in any given season is about as idle as speculation gets.

The past few years were not notable bonito seasons, despite early pronouncements by the bonito theorists that conditions were right for attracting the tasty little gamefish: "The water is real warm for this time. I figure we'll see a lot of bonito this year." "We've got a lot of bait holding. Should be a good year for bonito."

But the bonito never really showed up, particularly near the shore. Water temperatures are colder than normal this year, and bait seems to be scattered. Just what will the bonito season, which extends through the derby, be like?

For an answer I decided I would go outside the normal channels. Instead of calling tackle shops and speaking with fishermen, I decided it was time to broaden my perspective and speak with professionals who make it their business to predict the future.

I called Arlan Wise, a professional astrologer who writes a biweekly column for this newspaper. Arlan normally investigates the astrological signs in relation to their influence on people and businesses. But she was willing to give a quick opinion on what type of bonito season fishermen can expect.

"If I were going to give you an immediate answer," Arlan said, "I would say it was going to be better than the past two-and-a-half years."

I was impressed. Without knowing anything about the poor bonito fishing the past two years, Arlan had already made a pretty good prediction. She offered an explanation.

"Follow this," Arlan said. "Saturn, which is a planet that has to do with restrictions, this is where you see things are held in, has been in the sign of Pisces, which are the fish. Right? Water sign, ocean.

"The planet of restriction, you know limitation, in the sign of the fish, would by reflection probably talk about a tighter fishing season. So now that it has moved into another sign I would say there would be a release, and there would probably be more fish."

Arlan's explanation sounds as valid as some of the others I've heard in local tackle shops. Plus, I am looking forward to the reaction from Coop when I explain that the reason we are having a good bonito run is Saturn moved out of Pisces.

But I wanted to get one more opinion. With the confidence that my editor would support my journalistic quest, I called the La Toya Jackson Psychic Hotline and kept a nervous eye on the second hand as it swept around the dial at $3.99 per minute. I was greeted with a recorded message telling me I had to be 18 years of age, and that billing would begin in five seconds. "Beep."

A warm, friendly voice told me to dial the extension of my personal psychic, or wait for the next available one. I had already rung up $2 in charges and had not cast one fishing question when Lisa, at extension 315, came on the line. I was disappointed it was not La Toya, or even her brother Michael sitting in, but Lisa was pleasant.

"All right, dear," Lisa said, "have you ever had a reading before?"

A reasonable question, but I recognized the risks of idle chit-chat on The Times expense account and quickly got to the point.

"I am calling from the Martha's Vineyard Times, a newspaper," I told Lisa, "and I want a psychic prediction on what the bonito season will be like this year on Martha's Vineyard."

"The who thing?" Lisa said.

I explained, "It is a fish. Bonito are a fish, and I want to know what the fishing season will be like."

Lisa quickly recovered.

"Okay, all right, good enough. On Martha's Vineyard? All right," said Lisa. "I use the cards. The way they work is they tell you what's happenin', they also tell you what will happen, with an excellent rate of accuracy. All right, focusin' on that please, what's gonna happen' with the bo-nito season on Martha's Vineyard."

"How long does it last?" she asked.

I quickly told her "about three months," as we slid through my second $3.99 minute, and I began thinking about how I would explain this bill to the editor.

"And when does it begin?" asked Lisa.

About a week, I told her. I was impressed by her deliberate manner.

"All right," said Lisa, in a competent tone followed by what I could only interpret as the technical terms and techniques of her profession, "... kiyaba mona kibila ibayamona kushi ore kushi ore-bee ... bonito season ... bonito season ... Martha's Vineyard, over the next three months, light, nothing but light and progress, all right, cut it on the shuffle, cut the cards, all right, pulling the stack, now I'm putting the cards out here in this configuration that I've got 15 years of experience lookin' at ..."

I interrupted Lisa's action narrative right there.

"Okay," I said, "I need to know quickly, so I don't run up a bill." Lisa got to the point. "Slow! Slow as hell," Lisa said emphatically. "Slow as hell, that's my down and dirty quickie."

It looks like another typical bonito season.

The Fishing Mentality
Takes a Road Trip

A collision with a plow was not about to slow these anglers down. (June 1999)

THE STORY MAKES absolute sense to me. I am certain any fisherman who hears it will give an understanding nod. I am not sure anybody else would. But most fishermen readily acknowledge and take pride in the fact that they are part of a unique fraternity: One whose members pursue the sport of fishing undeterred by howling winds, crashing surf, driving rain — or even a 10-ton tandem axle Mack dump truck?

The Striped Bass Fly Rod Catch and Release Tournament, sponsored by the Martha's Vineyard Rod and Gun Club, attracts hundreds of fishermen each year. For many, the one-night tournament is an annual Vineyard fishing pilgrimage. It is also an opportunity to catch some fish and share some fun with fishermen from around the country.

Paul Fersen, Randy Carlson, and Matt Glerum work for the Orvis company in Manchester, Vt., and have been a large part of every catch and release tournament since it began eight years ago, both as supporters and participants. Last week, they packed Randy's new Pathfinder with fishing gear and left early Thursday morning for the approximately six-hour drive to Woods Hole ready to do some fishing.

Less than an hour after getting started, they decided to make the ritual stop for coffee and donuts. Randy was ready to make a left turn and stopped when the laws of physics intervened. Another driver sped around them and struck a woman in the car ahead of them who was just making a turn as well. A dump truck was coming the other way.

"He slammed into her rear end, pushed her into the opposite lane, and hit the dump truck," Paul says, "which knocked the rear end of the dump truck askew just enough so it came screaming into our lane."

He adds with a laugh, "It was kind of like a giant scientific experiment on Newton's laws, with all kinds of equal and opposite reactions going on."

But it is hard to be scientifically dispassionate when a 10-ton tandem axle dump truck with a plow harness is careening towards you. The three men sat in the car with their final thoughts.

"It was pretty interesting," Paul says in a bit of understatement. "I'm sitting there watching this silver grill get larger and larger in about two seconds."

If this were a made for television story about near-death experiences I could tell you that in the seconds before the impact Paul had a vision that changed him profoundly or that his whole life flashed before him. But this was a fishing trip to the Vineyard. What was on his mind with a Mack truck logo staring him in the face?

With a deep laugh Paul says, "This is the truth, the only thing I can think of is: this is really going to screw up my fishing trip."

The plow harness struck right on center and split the front end of the car wide open. The airbags deployed. The men were taken to a nearby hospital, where despite their bruises, they all appeared to be in one piece, much to the relief of Paul and Randy's worried wives, Mimi and Kathy, who quite naturally expected that their husbands would come home.

But this is a fishing story. Paul says they decided they could go home and sit under the covers while their wives fretted over them or still go fishing. It was an easy decision.

Paul explains with typical fisherman logic, "I mean nothing was injured to the point where we couldn't fish. So we got on the phone and called Mimi and Kathy and I said, okay, Mimi get my truck, go over to Kathy's house, pick Kathy up, so you've got something to ride back in, bring my truck down, we're outta here."

Most women who have been married to fishermen for any length of time are rarely surprised by the bouts of insanity the sport inspires or their husband's ability to rationalize why they go fishing in almost any conditions. But even Mimi and Kathy had to question the actions of the three men as they stood in the demo yard and unloaded fishing gear from Randy's mangled vehicle into Paul's truck.

But with their unanticipated three-hour delay there was still the problem of their 5:55 p.m. ferry reservation. Paul called the Steamship Authority office and explained the story of the car wreck and car switch and fishing trip to a boatline reservation clerk.

"The lady said, we'll try to do something for you, just bring a note from the hospital that you've been injured in a wreck."

They brought one of the hospital reports they had received which advised the men about how they should care for themselves after suffering a head injury. I asked Paul if it suggested anything about participating in a fly fishing tournament or recommended spending the night casting from the beach at Dogfish Bar. He admits with a laugh it did not. I can only assume the doctors were golfers.

On Sunday, at the tournament awards ceremony, we presented the three men with a special award, a copy of Minnesota governor Jesse Ventura's new book, "I Ain't Got Time to Bleed."

At least, not while there is time to fish.

Rene and Ton's Excellent Fishing Adventure

The "Dutch Guys" visit Martha's Vineyard.
(June 1999)

IT BEGAN WITH an E-mail this winter. A long electronic cast from the Netherlands from a Dutchman interested in fishing for striped bass on Martha's Vineyard. Rene Sehr had found The Martha's Vineyard Times web site and a summer's worth of fishing columns in the archive section.

Over the winter, in a series of E-mails, Rene, a freelance writer and shipping traffic controller for the port of Amsterdam, asked about the best months for fishing and fishing spots. Later messages updated me on his preparations and growing excitement.

In April, I received a copy of the Dutch fishing magazine, "Zee Hengelsport," with a story by Rene, "Einde Van een Tijdperk? Of Toch Niet!" Inside was a photograph of Rene, a "zeebaars specialist," holding a sea bass, which except for the stripes looked similar to a striped bass.

In the last E-mail message dated June 8, titled, "Only five days to go," Rene and his fishing buddy Ton Kalkman asked if they should bring a net. Waving the flag a bit I jokingly said they could not find one big enough for Vineyard stripers.

Their fishing trip got off to a slow start. A few small stripers from Lobsterville Beach. At Wasque they had fun with bluefish but no bass. But by the time Rene and Ton left the Vineyard last Sunday they had experienced the best the Vineyard has to offer and went home with memories of great fishing and American hospitality.

Rene and Ton got their first look at a real striper in the waters off the rocky shore of Squibnocket Point. Alex Preston, a Menemsha charter captain, knew about the E-mails and generously invited the "Dutch guys," out for an afternoon on his classic 29-foot Dyer bass boat. Both men said they were not prepared for the size of the fish that came over the transom.

"You see all the pictures but when Ton's fish came in I said, yes that's what we're here for," Rene said.

Ton added, "It's a living U-boat."

Both men agreed that Alex, who refused to accept any payment, was quite a guy. The next night Alley Moore and I introduced them to fishing with live eels from the beach at night. The following night they went back to the same spot on their own. It was an exciting and humbling experience for guys who consider themselves bass experts.

"I thought I knew everything about bass fishing," Rene said, "but here it's something completely different. I'm very addicted to bass fishing but these bass, there's no words to describe it."

Spreading his hands apart, then extending them as far as he could stretch, he said, "I'm used to this size bass, but then to see a cow like this." Describing his biggest fish of the night, Rene said, "I saw him come out, after he hit, wow, he took a run."

Ton, standing nearby was equally startled, "I thought he was falling over because I heard an immense splash. He said I've got one on, and bang. And then he took off, it's like starting an outboard motor you know, vroom, there he goes."

Ton added, "You can hear the bell from the bell buoy and it gives a special atmosphere you know a bit creepy but very exciting. And then the enormous splash."

(From left) Rene Sehr, Ton Kalkman and Alley Moore with one of several big striped bass caught in Menemsha Pond.

But while both fishermen have a wide ranging fishing vocabulary thanks to watching fishing videos and American fishing shows on satellite channels, and reading Cabela's and Bassmaster's catalogs, fishing with eels presented a unique moral dilemma.

Unquestionably, they agreed the live eels worked. But the technique of impaling an eel so it remains alive went against deeply ingrained ethics. On the second night they killed the eels first before using them.

Ton explained, "We in Holland have a very different thought about it. Killing animals, we're not used to it because we don't have a lot of nature in Holland so if we have a little piece of nature we preserve it as much as possible."

He said, "When we grow up they teach us when you see an animal in the wild you have to preserve it because we have only a few of them, but I must be realistic, if it [live eels] is a good way, it is a good way."

In Holland, Ton said, there is an animal ambulance. "When a dog is hit by a car or a cat or even a seagull you can call and they come when you call, even in the middle of the night and they don't say, oh it's a seagull, they say, oh my goodness a seagull is hurt. I think that's a little bit different here. There is a lot of space."

I assured Ton we have an animal ambulance for deer. It's called the pickup truck.

Midweek, they returned to the Tivoli Inn in Oak Bluffs where they were staying, with a big bass for the owner, Lori Katsounakis. It was after midnight, but Lori was just getting back from a walk with her friend, Curtis Hopps, a former Derby champ.

To their surprise, Curt immediately started cleaning the fish and Lori reheated a striped bass stuffed with scallops, garlic and onions she had made earlier in the evening. It was Rene and Ton's first opportunity to eat striped bass.

The fishing atmosphere and acceptance of recreational fishing is very different than that in Holland. Rene said one night he was fishing from the beach at night in the winter. "Some woman came wading through the very cold water just to ask whether we were trying to commit suicide or something."

Commercial fishing, mostly with gill nets, largely goes unregulated. Quotas are the only limit and shore fishermen are often part of a commercial "black market" that is fueled by prices in excess of $6 per pound for a whole uncleaned fish. Catch and release is almost unknown.

"Very few people return the fish" Rene said, "they say why catch and release because the gill nets are waiting."

Both men were impressed with the hospitality they encountered everywhere they went, particularly in the Island's tackle shops. Ton, searching for the right words, said, "All the people, especially the people involved in fishing, they are so open, so friendly, we do like American people over in Holland, of course that's no problem."

"But," he said, "we have a certain thought about America, everything's bigger, better, but now we came here and this was my first time in the US and everyone is so friendly especially in the shops."

Ton added, "I think it was a real eye opener I think you call that."

The following Letter to the Editor was published in The Martha's Vineyard Times on Sept. 29, 2001:

An Attack on Freedom and Humanity

To the Editor:

I miss the knowledge of your language to express what I felt last week when I heard the news.

Although I have been in the US only three times, when visiting Martha's Vineyard, it felt as if my heart was hit by a hammer.

At the moment I heard about the disaster that had taken place I was touring in the highlands of Scotland. There was an instant feeling of "this is not true" and even when I saw the images on the TV I couldn't believe it ... but sadly it was true.

What can I say?

I only want you people there to know that although this monstrous act of human madness took place in New York, we here in Holland feel it as an attack on everything that stands for freedom and humanity, so that makes it an attack on us all.

Be assured our heartfelt sympathy is with all our fishing friends on the Island and all our fellow Americans in these dark days.

Hope to see you all next year.

Ton Kalkman, "a fellow fisherman"
The Netherlands

Hospital ER Got This
Angler Off the Hook

Hook removal is a specialty of the Martha's Vineyard Hospital
(August 1999)

IN THE COURSE of reporting on the Fourth of July weekend, I
stopped at the Martha's Vineyard Hospital emergency room. It
had been a normal holiday weekend, said a nurse, who recounted
a litany of the usual summer accident fare, including a fisherman
who needed a fishing hook removed from his body.

I learned that fishermen misplace fishing hooks often enough
so that a special fish hook removal kit is kept at the ready in the
emergency room. I made a mental note to write about it. I imagined a small box containing a variety of specialized instruments.

The Saturday before last, I was fishing with Andy Peterson
when his eleven-year-old son, Billy, buried a treble hook in the
back of his young head. I figured it was as good a time as any to
get my story.

We'd been fishing for small stripers from the shore of Tisbury
Great Pond in the early evening. Billy was casting a Striper Swiper,
a plug that splashes along the surface and normally comes armed
with a forward and rear treble hook. I'd removed the forward
hook, a precaution I often take to avoid accidents, but this evening
it wasn't enough.

With the plug hanging a little too far from the rod tip, Billy wound up for a cast. The plug swung around and hit him in the back of the head. One of the three hook points buried itself just behind his left ear.

I was up the beach when I noticed dad and son having some sort of a problem. I hoped it was just a line tangle, but the blue and white plug hanging from the back of Billy's head suggested it was not that simple. I cut the fishing line and opened the eye of the hook to remove the plug body and get it out of the way. There was only a dribble of blood and I hoped I might be able to pull the hook out. But it was under the skin and deeply buried.

Billy maintained the demeanor of a Spartan. There was not a whimper, not a tear, not a complaint out of this kid. I thought of my eight-year-old daughter and the time I removed a small splinter from her leg. Her screams gave the impression that I was operating without anesthetic. But Billy was completely nonplussed, and as we walked up the beach he admitted that with three older brothers he was used to a few knocks.

On the way to the hospital I asked if it hurt. "No," he said. "Did it hurt when it happened? I asked, searching for a reaction.

"It just felt kind of weird," he said.

At the emergency room registration table Andy told a large, cheery woman taking insurance information that he was there for hook removal. Billy dutifully turned his head to show off the large treble neatly protruding from his scalp.

"Yup," she said eyeing the problem matter-of-factly, "we can do that."

A young couple sitting on the couch waiting to have their particular problem attended to looked over. The woman saw the hook and nudged her partner. Unable to contain herself she started to laugh. Really, what could you say? It looked pretty funny, and for his part, Billy was just interested in getting a Coke from a machine in the hall. That accomplished, he sat down to watch a football game on the TV in the waiting room.

Andy, a labor lawyer by trade, the father of eight kids by profession, called his wife, Ann Marie, to let her know what was going on. But you don't raise six boys and two girls without a certain equanimity when it comes to the trials involved with raising kids. He acted like it was just another day at the office.

"It looks like you got mixed up with where that hook is supposed to be," Dr. Gerry Yukevich said as he came into the treatment room, "Let's size up what we've got here."

Billy lay down on the stretcher and Dr. Yukevich gently pushed and prodded the hook. Slowly he explained to the young boy what was going to happen next.

"I'm going to numb the spot and it's going to sting for ten to fifteen seconds," he explained to Billy. "Then I'm going to put something on it to clean it. I'm going to try and poke it through and clip off the point where the barb is."

"Okay?" he asked.

"Okay," said Billy.

A nurse brought in a small, green package with a taped label that said "Hook Removal Kit." Spread out on the table, its contents were no more exotic than a small vial of lidocaine — a local anesthetic — a syringe, and a pair of what appeared to be electrician's vise grips with a side wire cutter.

According to Dr. Yukevich, quite often it is easier and less damaging to the surrounding tissue to push a barbed hook through than to try and pull it out. In some cases, an incision is necessary. But the key is to know the anatomy of the hooked area so there is no damage to nerves or arteries. It is also essential to be as sterile as possible. Infection is always a concern.

"We try to minimize the pain and do it quickly," said the doctor. With the nurse reassuring the young boy, Dr. Yukevich gave him a shot to numb the area. Later, Billy admitted the pain almost made him cry. Quite an admission from a kid who up to that point hadn't said "ouch."

But the procedure to push the hook through, clip it, and back it out did not go smoothly. The doctor couldn't quite get the barb through, and as he struggled with the hook, Andy and I looked at each other with a mutual expression of "yikes!"

"Is it still in my head? Billy asked.

"Still in your head, buddy," the doctor said calmly.

Finally, after some further maneuvering, he clipped the point of the hook with a loud "ping," and backed it out.

Billy didn't get a fish that night, but he did get to keep the barb-less hook and stop for a big ice cream cone on the way home.

But not every hook-related fishing injury ends with an ice cream cone. In one case, a man struck in the head by a Kastmaster, a heavy metal jig, was sent to a Boston area hospital for neurosurgery. Eye and hand injuries can also be problematic. Some cautious fishermen prefer to use single hooks rather than trebles, and crush down the barbs. Large swimming plugs with multiple treble hooks can pose a real risk if the fish suddenly jumps.

That is what happened many years ago to Ed Jerome, Edgartown School principal and derby president. Ed said he was reaching for a bluefish he'd hooked on a Rebel when the fish jumped and buried a hook deeply into his thumb. Ed went up the beach where Gerry Westover, a doctor, was fishing. He normally traveled with his medical bag but not that night.

Over walked Cooper Gilkes. He told Ed he'd learned a new technique from the folks who make Trilene fishing line. It involved looping a piece of fishing line around the shank and pushing down on the hook to depress the barb. Theoretically, a quick yank would then pull the hook out the same way it went in.

"So, Coop came up and said, 'Wait a second I just learned about this new technique from Trilene,'" Ed said, laughing as he remembered the story.

"Coop's going, 'Honest Ed, it'll work, it'll work."

"So there's about five guys on the beach now and they're holding my arm and my hand and Coop goes, 'Ready?' He yanked on it and I went down to my knees; I tell you I was in so much pain I almost threw up."

At that point, Ed must have been delirious because he let Coop, or "Dr. Yank" as he now refers to him, give it two more tries. Then he drove himself to the hospital.

It being the derby, Ed caught the first Chappy ferry and was fishing the gut for bonito and albies when the other guys came off the beach. At the awards ceremony that year, Ed was presented with a big trophy of a thumb with a hook in it.

Asked about the Trilene technique, one emergency room professional said he had seen it in books and heard people talk about. But he added, "I've never seen it work."

A Fisherman's Friend
Seals His Fate

A cry in the night is something to laugh about when you are a bass fisherman.
(June 2000)

IT IS A classic theme. Famed Japanese film director Akira Kurosawa used it when he first won worldwide critical acclaim with the movie Rashomon. Several different individuals give their own twist as each retells the story of the same event. It is one of those movies film critics rave about and guys rent to impress a date.

According to film critic James Berardinelli, "Many people watch Rashomon with the intent of piecing together a picture of what really occurred. However, the accounts are so divergent that such an approach seems doomed to futility."

I'm not a film critic (although I do like Kurosawa's action flicks) but I could not help but think of Rashomon as I listened to different versions of a story about a fisherman's encounter with a seal.

The first version I heard was delivered by builder Joe Chapman. In Joe's version, he and a buddy he did not identify made the long walk out to go bass fishing at night at Squibnocket Point on the Saturday night of Memorial Day weekend. That's when he had an encounter with a seal.

According to Joe, he was startled but steadfast in the face of the marine leviathan. Deciding to probe the depths of the human soul and sensing a fishing column, I asked artist Andrew Moore, a friend of Joe's, to give him a call and see what version of the story he got. According to Andrew, Joe told him he was casting from a rock and saw his fishing partner, Ned Casey, change locations, so after a little time he also decided to find a new rock.

"So he started to move and heard this hissing sound," Andrew said. Walking a little farther and carrying his fishing rod tip forward he heard the sound again, almost like a hissing, but he thought it was his waders rubbing together.

When he heard the sound again he flipped on his light, and in front of him was a seal which promptly nipped the end of Joe's custom surf rod built by Stevie Morris' grandfather, Dick, of Dick's Tackle Shop fame. Joe didn't realize his rod had been shortened until he walked out to another rock to fish some more.

Andrew asked Joe if he was frightened. Joe told him he was a little bit when he heard the noise, but when he saw it was a little harbor seal, he was not that intimidated.

Andrew added, "But he did mention they have some serious teeth."

Joe told Andrew that Ned had been having a good time with the story and confided to him, "I'm sure Nelson's going to get ahold of it, and it'll probably be in the paper."

In fact, Ned, the unidentified fishing buddy when Joe told me the story, had already been by to visit me at the office.

Ned, a carpenter, told a slightly different version. He said both of them were fishing in Steve's Memorial Day weekend tournament and decided to go out to Squibnocket together. Ned said he caught a few small fish when Joe yelled to him that he was going to move around the point. Ned said he was going to give it a few more minutes and then they would meet.

"It was just black, right about quarter past nine, just black" said Ned, "and I could see Joe wading through, all I could see is his light bouncing around."

Ned said he kept a watch on Joe just to make sure he got to shore okay. Joe got back to shore when Ned said, "All of a sudden I hear this yelling and screaming, 'heh-heh, heyyy, yaaah' I'm lookin' around and thinking he fell in."

Ned said he looked dead behind him in the direction of the shouts and watched as the beam from Joe's headlamp flashed wildly in different directions as Joe continued to shout.

"All I could hear him saying is, 'seal, seal,'" Ned said. "So I climb off the rock and I'm going in there and he yells, 'Look out! Look out! A seal just attacked me.'"

Joe told Ned that a seal grabbed ahold of his fishing rod and broke the tip right off. Ned, in disbelief, asked, "What are you talkin' about?"

Joe said, "I heard this hissing sound, and I didn't know what it was. I thought it was my waders rubbing up against my jacket, and I turned around, and I looked in front of me, and this seal grabbed onto my fishing rod, and he wouldn't let go, and he snapped my fishing rod."

The steadfast (based on his retelling) Ned Casey asked, "Where's this seal?"

Ned said, "I thought it was going to be this big, huge gray seal, you know. I looked around the rock and it's this little harbor seal, about three feet long, you know with those big ol puppy dog eyes, you know what I mean, trying to get away from us."

As Ned recounted the story, Joe wanted to leave, but Ned wanted to continue fishing, so Joe decided to stay as well.

"It was the night of the killer seal," Ned said with a laugh. Mindful that I would be retelling the story, Ned, a true fishing buddy, offered a few words of editorial encouragement on his friend's behalf.

"Nelson," he said as he walked out the door, "play it up big, make Joe look like a real schmuck."

A Fisherman's Inner Voice
Cries Out in Vain

It was not a Hallmark Card moment for this father and husband.
(June 2000)

EVERY FISHING SEASON I find myself relearning familiar lessons. It is not that I forget. Now and then I just have to be reminded about some of the basic rules of fishing and life.

For example, never try to force a fish out of the surf, always sharpen your hooks, and be sure to listen to a little voice screaming "it's time to go" if you have promised your wife and daughter you will be home to cook a lobster dinner for Mother's Day.

On Mother's Day, Alley Moore suggested we go out fishing for a few hours. Alley and his wife, Michelle, and another couple had 8:30 pm reservations at the Sweet Life Café for Mother's Day. Alley said he had to be back by 7 pm, which gave me an excuse to take my time monitoring responsibilities casually.

Doing my part to honor motherhood, I bought three lobsters and a couple of pounds of littlenecks and told my wife, Norma, and nine-year-old daughter, Marlan, I would prepare dinner.

Tom Robinson had wisely declined to go fishing with us. Tom explained that on their own, boys could not be counted on to remember Mother's Day, and it was in his own self-interest to make sure that his three sons did something for their mother.

He pointed out that because I had a daughter it was different. That is true, very true. One of the more intriguing aspects of watching my daughter grow up is that from time to time I see the kernel of a future wife and mother.

About 4 pm Alley and I headed to the flats near Eel Pond in Edgartown to look for some stripers. Bass fishing is generally best at night, but when the fish are on the move they will often hit during the day. Still, after more than an hour of casting it was clear the fish were either not there or uninterested.

It was about 6 pm and I suggested we stop at the Bend-in-the-Road Beach and see if there were any bluefish before we headed home. My second cast drew a powerful strike.

The bluefish were there in force. I took a hookless plug and tried to draw fish to the beach while Alley cast his fly rod. It was exciting to watch two or three fish pursue the plug then shout to Alley to drop the fly in front of the charging fish.

At some point in all this activity the little voice yelled to me, but I ignored it. I have ignored it before. In that way fishermen are really sick people.

Besides, I knew Alley had to be home at 7 pm and assumed he would say something. But he never did. I took my fly rod and Alley began drawing the fish in. The sun got lower in the sky.

In deference to the little voice I told Alley I was ready to go whenever he was. Alley suggested that perhaps we had better get going. But the urgency of our situation could not penetrate the fishing fog surrounding our brains.

Alley began to reel in his fly so we could pack up. "You know what that means, don't you," I said to Alley. Sure enough, a blue hit the fly. Now I could safely tell Alley, "C'mon, break that fish off, we have to get going."

I didn't dare look at my watch but the sun was at the horizon. We arrived at Alley's and I could see Michelle and the other couple waiting inside. Alley wanted me to stop in at his house as if it involved some social nicety and not a desperate attempt to deflect responsibility. But I have tried that before myself and this time I had not a moment to waste. I tossed his stuff unceremoniously out of my car onto the lawn and took off.

During the short but very long ride from Oak Bluffs to Vineyard Haven, I had a familiar conversation with myself. For the most part I wondered what the hell was I thinking. Clearly I was not thinking and that is one of the many curious things about fishermen. We rarely devote even a portion of the time we spend analyzing tides into the predicaments we slide into because of fishing.

My wife is a wonderful woman who has learned to live with a fisherman. She does not believe anything I say if I have a fishing rod in my hand and laughs out loud at any suggestion of responsible behavior on my part during the derby. But on Mother's Day she did expect me to be home to cook the lobsters.

I walked in the door with a brave face. I was met with stony stares and silence from Norma and Marlan. Quickly I began preparing our dinner, trying to think of something to say that would distinguish me from a crustacean in need of being dropped into a boiling pot of water.

Norma told me later with some amusement that as I had pulled into the driveway Marlan had asked her, "Mom, how are we going to punish him?"

After a moment's thought, Marlan came up with her own answer: "I know, mom," she said, "We'll give him the silent treatment."

I should have known.

Vineyard Provides a Memorable Family Fishing Trip

At the last moment, Christin Carotta of Louisville, Ky. joined her dad.
(May 2001)

THE BEST FISH we catch are never caught just once. There is the actual moment when the fish is brought to the beach, and then there are the memories of fish we have caught, and moments we have shared with others, which come flooding back, sometimes under the light of a full moon far from the sound of the surf.

A few sharp-eyed Jersey fishermen plugging away in the rain, wind, and pounding surf last Wednesday discovered the fish. By the fourth day of the South Beach blitz, there would be fewer stripers, many more fishermen, and some families with very special memories of fishing on Martha's Vineyard.

I did not hear about it until late Friday afternoon and only because I happened to stop at Coop's on my way to drop off a package in Edgartown.

"Let's go," Coop said as I walked in the door, "it started about this time yesterday." A pair of 11-foot surf rods were already on his truck.

"What started?" I asked.

Coop looked at me, surprised that I hadn't already heard. "The bass blitz," he said. A school of big fish had been feeding off South

Beach, a stretch of sand on the Atlantic facing side of the Island. The fish were discovered Wednesday.

I hesitated, held back by a sense of responsibility and prior work commitments. He told me that when he'd come over the dune on Thursday the first thing he saw was four big bass chasing plugs on the surface and fishermen hooked up along the beach. I questioned whether yesterday's fishing would repeat itself.

"Ben just came back with a keeper," he said. "He's cleanin' it in the back."

I made a quick call and jumped in the truck. When we arrived I was happy to see Janet Messineo standing on the beach casting. I took her presence there as sure a sign of big fish in the area as diving terns. But she wasn't having much luck, a fact that did not appear to dampen her spirits.

"Beats workin'," she told me with a smile.

Other surf regulars like the venerable Don Mohr, Marsh Bryan, and Paul Schultz were plugging away with varied success — a few blues, some nice bass — but none were catching fish like Rick Zane. Wielding an 11-foot rod he'd built himself from a Ron Arra Lamiglas blank, Rick, from New Jersey and on vacation with his two brothers, father, uncle, and young nephew, was propelling his plug further than most and out to where the fish were lying in wait.

The Zanes had grown up surf fishing the South Jersey shore around Barnegat Light with their father, Charles. This trip was the family's 14th annual fishing pilgrimage to the Vineyard.

"Eat, sleep, and fish, that's what we do," Dave Zane said, describing the family's three-week vacation itinerary as he took a break from casting. On Thursday, he said, the family tally was 84 striped bass, 83 of them keepers more than 28 inches long. "All of them are still swimming, except one we kept for dinner," he said.

I never had a hook up. On Saturday afternoon I returned and it was clear the word was out. More than 40 fishermen were lined up along a short section of beach, all casting as far as they could. Janet was also back.

"I'm due today," she told me, between puffs of her cigarette. "I got all my bad luck out of the way yesterday." Her sense of impending good fortune increased when a bird crapped on her truck window (a story for another day).

Most of the fishermen standing on the beach were separated by an average distance of eight feet. Some stood even closer. Given the fact that most of them were using fishing rods more than nine feet long to toss teardrop-shaped hard plastic lures weighing two to three ounces, I estimated that the official fishing concussion probability index was 6 on a scale of 1 to 5.

As did most of those fishing Saturday, I had missed the best action. Fish were still being caught but not as many as on the previous days when bass were chasing surface plugs. This day most of the fish were taken in brief exciting spurts of action.

The focus of the action was a sandbar that had formed approximately 100 yards from shore, running parallel to South Beach at the end of the right fork in Katama. For experienced striper fishermen like Rick and the Zane brothers, the bar had looked like classic striper territory Wednesday and a good place to try a cast.

Bass are attracted to areas of white water and swirling current caused when waves break over a bar that is separated from the beach by a channel or trough. Stripers use their broad powerful tail to hold in the current, lying in wait to pick off trapped or disoriented baitfish.

The South Beach blitz was no place for short rods or short casts. The fish were way out. A thick, broad band of weeds along the beach presented another obstacle, draping fishing lines and otherwise adding weight and difficulty to the job of pulling a big bass through the surf and up onto the beach.

Christin Carotta, on the Vineyard with her family for one week of the family's two-week fishing vacation, was undeterred by

Thursday's wind, rain, and surf. On Saturday she was still plugging away, earning the respect of the regulars.

Her family, including her dad, mom, brother, and grandmother, had traveled to the Vineyard from Louisville, Ky., for the family's annual fishing vacation, usually two to three weeks long. Christin, a sophomore from Loyola, had decided to join them.

Christin Carotta holds up a big striped bass
caught on South Beach.

In among a line of fishermen Saturday, Christin took a solid hit. She stayed with the fish as the big striper started to take out line and head down the beach, walking in front of other fishermen on the beach. Many offered words of encouragement as her arms began to ache with the effort. She slid the striper up onto the beach, a beautiful 40-inch striped bass. Don Mohr walked over and gave her a congratulatory kiss on the cheek.

Christin walked back behind the line of admiring fishermen carrying her fish to shouts of "nice fish," and "good job." She was walking on the sand. Her father, Mike Carotta, was walking six feet above the beach.

Let ESPN interview the tennis dads and their pouty, spoiled brats; I'll take fishing dads anytime. Mike told me that his daughter had been fishing all over Chappy all week with just one bluefish to show for the effort. "We're talkin' six-hour days in the rain," he pointed out emphatically.

He said the family had come to the bar the previous two nights and even tried their luck at 5:30 in the morning, but had had no success. He said that on Thursday his daughter got knocked down by a wave but got back up and kept on casting. He related proudly, "Coop came over to me and said, 'You've got some partner.'"

Christin wondered who it was that had given her a peck on the cheek. Told it was Don Mohr, she smiled.

"This was her last half-hour of fishin'," Mike said, "she goes back to school tomorrow. It's a fitting end to a great trip."

Adding some perspective, he said, "We're talkin' a 3.8 student here."

Mike said he had not caught a keeper bass in 10 years. Clearly, at that moment, he couldn't care less. His little girl had caught a big fish and that was all that mattered.

Mike said that Christin had always been a part of the family fishing trip. But no matter how dads wish it would not happen, little girls have a way of growing up.

Mike said that two years ago, he and Christin had spent the evening fishing under a full moon beneath Cape Poge Light. She had just graduated from high school and two months later was due to go off to college.

Mike wondered if that had been their last fishing trip. The following year the family was unable to make the Vineyard trip.

But this spring, with plans made for the annual Vineyard fishing vacation, Mike got a telephone call. The moon was full in the night sky.

"I saw the moon, too, dad," Christin told her father.

"Can I come up early in May and go fishing?"

Cagey Vermonters Teach
Islanders a Thing or Two

There may be no striped bass in the Green Mountain state but there are fishermen.
July 2006

I FIGURE THERE ARE lots of black flies in Vermont, maple syrup, cows I suppose, cheddar cheese, expatriate New Yorkers wearing clean plaid shirts, trout, and no big striped bass. But the Green Mountain state is known for producing enterprising citizens, notables like Ethan Allen and characters Larry, Darryl, and Darryl on the popular Bob Newhart Show. So leave it to a pair of Vermonters to teach local Islanders a thing or two about fishing for bass on their own doorstep.

With customers flowing into Menemsha fish markets in search of the freshest fish and the up-Island charter fleet leaving the harbor to hunt for big striped bass, Mark Younger and his father James set out chairs behind Larsen's Fish Market and pulled in big fish after big fish at all hours of the day right from the dock. The biggest fish was 55 inches long and weighed a whopping 47 pounds.

Day after day another man fishing from the dock caught nothing. What was the secret? The Vermonters had stumbled upon bait that was irresistible to striped bass.

I tracked down James this week at his home in Brattleboro and asked him about his Vineyard vacation. I said that I had heard that he and his son had caught an impressive number of fish. He spoke in the flat accent and laconic manner of a native Vermonter.

James likes to fish "all the time" he said. Most of the fishing he does is for trout, often in the portion of the Deerfield River that runs through Massachusetts. He is a retired cook. Mark is a contractor.

"How old a fellow are you? I asked James. "Seventy-three, today," he told me.

Mark's girlfriend's mother owns a house in Vineyard Haven, he said. He and Mark traveled to the Vineyard the end of June and stayed until July 8. It was their second trip. "We went down last year and we caught one fish," he told me.

Why did they decide to fish off the dock behind Larsen's? "Well, we wanted to go out in a charter boat and they want $400 and something and you're only allowed two fish. That's a pretty expensive fish," he said.

"So we were in the fish market gettin' something to eat and someone said try it right off the dock, so we did, and it worked pretty good."

In a later conversation James expanded on the decision to first fish off the dock. "My dad's kind of handicapped and he could not go a lot of places so I asked the guy in the fish market where I could take my old man to catch some striper and he says, try right off the back of the dock. And I said, really? He says, yeah right off the back. So I brought a chair down for him and sure enough he caught one. He was happier than hell."

Not surprisingly, when their first fishing foray on this year's vacation, a trip out to the beach at Wasque, came up dry, they decided to go back to the dock. And it was absolutely amazing, said James excitedly.

But just how amazing was it really? You decide.

"What were you using for bait?" I asked James.

"Farm-raised salmon," he said matter-of-factly.

Had that come from an Islander I would have laughed. Had I been having a conversation standing in a Vermont general store I would have suspected he was putting me on. But talking to this Vermonter on the phone, I knew he was telling me the truth.

"From the market?" I asked.

"Yup."

Island striper fishermen use live eels. They use squid, clams, scup, herring, menhaden and sand eels. Serge de Somov, the legendary "mad Russian" who won the Martha's Vineyard Striped Bass and Bluefish Derby in 1963, 1964, 1965 and again in 1969 was rumored to use lobsters for bait. But salmon, that was a new one on me.

I checked with the Stop and Shop. Salmon was going for $5.99 a pound. At Island tackle shops eels cost between $18 and $24 a dozen. Squid is $2 per pound.

I asked James what gave them the idea to use salmon for bait.

"Well, we went to the fish market and bought every damn thing there was," said James. "We bought squid, we bought herring, heck we bought everything but swordfish. So we were at this supermarket at the Island there, Stop and Shop, and we bought a couple of packages of farm-raised salmon there and we tried it and it worked marvelous."

I wondered if maybe it was a question of having leftovers from dinner. "No," James assured me, "We bought it for bait, not to eat it."

Mark expanded on the choice of bait. "We tried it the year before when we weren't catching anything and we caught a couple the day before we were going to leave. So we said the next year when we came down we were going to try it again and it was absolutely amazing – 55 inches long, 47 pounds!"

Mark said he and his dad caught their two-bass limit each day. But the biggest thrill was hooking the forty-pounder, an accomplishment any veteran surf man would be proud of.

It was about 3 pm. Mark felt a fish take the bait and set the hook. The fish took off for the inlet he said like a jet plane. After a 25-minute battle he had it at the dock. He had to borrow a net big enough to land the fish. Meanwhile a large crowd gathered. James said it seemed like the inside of a football stadium.

Captain Dick Vincent of the Flashy Lady, an experienced Menemsha charter captain and a man who knows how to catch big bass, was duly impressed. Dick got on his marine radio. "He said you ain't going to believe what those Vermonters got."

When the Vermonters first started fishing the regulars along the dock had told them they would not catch bass during the daytime. Mark said there was one older fisherman who became increasingly irritated. Day after day he caught nothing while the father and son duo kept pulling in fish. But Islanders are adaptive.

"Finally, he used salmon and he caught a couple too," Mark said. "Within four days everybody was using salmon."

Mark asked me if I had ever used salmon. I said I had not.

"Well let me tell you they hit it," he said.

Mark said he is planning to return to the Vineyard this fall to fish the derby with his family and co-workers.

"We are all going to be there," said Mark. "So tell 'em they gotta make room on the dock, the Vermonters are coming."

Fisherman Welcomes the
Return of Mission Control

The five-week absence of my wife was no fishing vacation.
(August 2008)

I HAVE NOTHING TO say about fishing. Not a word to report. I have not been fishing and can pass on no firsthand information.

I have spent the last week feverishly raking dirt, digging dirt, cutting vegetation, watering everything in sight, vacuuming (not so much of that) and sweating, mostly sweating. I had lots of projects to accomplish in a short span of time.

On Sunday my wife and daughter return from a five-week adventure in New York City. This is very good news for Oscar the goldfish, Tashmoo the dog, and me the husband.

Some people thought the absence of my wife, Norma, meant I would spend lots of time fishing. That was not the case.

The astronauts would be lost without mission control. In my house and the house of many fishermen, the wife is mission control (Lela Gilkes is the equivalent of Gene Kranz the head of mission control in Apollo 13). Wives are the support system.

I took a young friend out fishing during the VFW Fluke Derby. He and I were a team. I told his mom I would attend to sandwiches. The morning of the tournament I prepared sandwiches with the only ingredients in my refrigerator. Our day's rations were cream cheese and bacon sandwiches.

Some chef in a fancy California eatery could probably pass off bacon and cream cheese as new American cuisine, but had my wife been home there is no way she would have let me feed that kid such a concoction. Mission control would have made sure we had roast beef or turkey.

Norma has been in New York looking after our daughter while she attended a summer theater program for teens. That left me on my own.

Ask a fisherman if he appreciates his wife, and unless he has already engaged a divorce lawyer, he will say yes. We think we appreciate our wives, and our wives all think we do not, or at least not to the degree that we should.

It is not easy being married to a fisherman. Over the course of our married life my wife has found a striped bass in the bathtub surrounded by ice, live eels in the refrigerator vegetable bin and dead, decomposing and reeking eels in the basement.

My wife no longer agrees to attend any social event if I will be fishing prior to the engagement. Past experience has shown her that I am not to be trusted when I say I will be home in plenty of time to get ready.

I knew her summer absence meant an adjustment. I know how to operate the washing machine and dryer, run the vacuum and iron a shirt (not that I tried, and my wardrobe reflected it). And I am perfectly capable of going shopping for myself. It had just been a while, and my timing was off.

The first week Norma was gone I kept forgetting that I needed to stop at the store. When a married guy says he had eggs for dinner, it is a pretty good indication that his wife is away.

With Norma gone, my responsibilities included her goldfish, Oscar, and our very old Lab, Tashmoo. Oscar did not need a lot of tending, a few sprinkles of dried bait every few days and occasional water replenishment.

Tashmoo is another story. Tashmoo's life revolves around his dog bowl and his bladder. And Labs, in addition to their many wonderful qualities, can tell time. Tashmoo knows when it is time to eat. That meant I needed to be home at 7 am, and I needed to be home at 5 pm. That put a crimp in any boating plans. Luckily the heat and humidity kept Tashmoo in a flatline stupor that allowed me an hour or so on the upper end of his schedule.

Although Tashmoo has eaten the same dry, brown pellet-like food his entire life, he reacts to every meal as though it were his first. My menu was more varied. One of my assigned tasks while Norma was away was to eat items from our basement freezer that had missed the household rotation and had a date ending in 06 or 07. These are the kinds of things husbands are good at.

Fishermen are very good at living off the land (convenience store and take-out establishments). Years ago, before I was married, I survived during the derby on pizza slices and candy bars.

Cooking for one creates logistical challenges. For me it was the vegetable. To solve the problem, I substituted those one-serving plastic containers of applesauce that come in eight-packs and have a shelf life similar to plutonium.

The absence of my wife and teenage daughter meant that I had complete control over the television. I could now watch shows of all kinds, including those that begin with a warning that some material may not be suitable for all audiences, which provide dramatic scenes of animals, fish and people eating other animals, fish and people, or any combination thereof.

One evening I watched Michael Caine and Jack Hawkins battle an army of Zulu warriors — probably the tenth time I have seen the film "Zulu." Norma would have had something to say about that. I could have spent the past five weeks fishing in my spare time. Norma expected that.

When Norma returns on Sunday she will find a small stone retaining wall in place of an eroding bank and weeds. She will find a small patio in place of weeds that passed for a lawn. And she will find a bluestone driveway newly expanded so my boat will not be in the way. That required removing one of her flowerbeds. I know it will be a surprise.

I look forward to fishing. Mission control is back.

Casting Into a Sea of Memories for a Daughter Now Grown Up

A fisherman marks the passage of time.
(August 2009)

THERE IS A photo next to my desk. It is of my daughter Marlan when she was about eight years old. In it she is holding a fluke by hooking her finger into the fish's gills. As I recall she was unimpressed and somewhat reluctant to hold the fish. But I insisted and she relented.

I find great pleasure in the act of fishing. The rewards are many, whether I am walking up Lobsterville Beach looking for the telltale swirl of a striped bass, or drifting in a boat bottom bouncing bait for fluke.

So it was only natural I suppose that I hoped my daughter Marlan would also. I think every fisherman who becomes a dad has that idea. If childhood interests developed by way of osmosis Marlan would have shown an early interest in fishing.

There is another photo on the wall to my left. I am standing in front of Coop's holding a big bluefish I caught one morning off South Beach about one week after the Derby ended. I have a thicker head of hair than I do now and an unseen Norma is standing behind me perching Marlan on my shoulder. She is about six-months-old dressed in a cap and sweater Norma had knit.

I am not sure what the inspiration was for that photo but Marlan wears a stunned expression. She was too young to express outrage at the embarrassing actions of her father then. That would come later and regularly once she became a teenager.

From time to time, when Marlan was still a baby I would combine parenting responsibilities with fishing. Like the morning I put Marlan in a backpack and cast a spinning rod along Lobsterville Beach. I was limited in my ability to chase fish but it was fun to have her along for the ride.

Above that photo there is one of Marlan, about four, sitting at my fly-tying vise one winter evening. She looks a little irritated because she did not want to be interrupted by dad.

Marlan had watched me tying flies and was attracted to the bright feathers and colored tinsel I assembled into imitations of baitfish. Aha, I thought, an opportunity to tap into Marlan's creativity and love of crafts. I imagined her becoming a skilled fly-tier and standing one day in a stream fly casting in my imagined remake of the famous casting scene in the movie that introduced the beauty of fly fishing to the public, "A River Runs Through It."

I set up the vise and covered the point of the bare hook with cork. Then I set about to carefully instruct Marlan on how to tie a fly. She would have none of it. What she wanted to do was take clumps of tinsel and feather and wrap them together and that is what she did despite my exasperation. Thinking back now, I regret I cared so much about whether she was learning anything, or even whether she was wasting tinsel and feathers. I would gladly part with all of it now to have those hours back.

One year I was able to cajole Marlan into waking up early and going to the rod and gun club spring trout derby. It is an annual event that attracts hundreds of Island kids and has produced generations of fishermen.

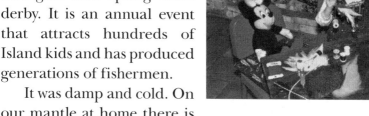

It was damp and cold. On our mantle at home there is a photo of by the pond of Marlan hugging Angela George, our neighbor and one of the many girls with whom Marlan would experience all of the fun and emotional anguish of growing up in a small community.

Marlan caught a small catfish and insisted she be allowed to bring it home and show it to mom. I agreed. Catfish are hardy and the fish made the trip in a bucket to our bathtub without much apparent harm. Mom was suitably impressed and I said it was time to release the fish. Marlan was adamant that she be allowed to keep it with her as a pet. I attempted to reason with her. We needed to release the fish, I said.

"Remember in the movie ET, how the kids help ET return home," I told her.

"Dad," Marlan said in her direct little way, "those were boys."

I still chuckle at her reasoning. Marlan has always been every bit a girl and drawn a sharp distinction between the thought processes of boys and girls.

When she was a little older I bundled her up in warm clothes and took her duck hunting. Sitting in a makeshift duck blind with our dog Tashmoo she made imaginary tea with some twigs and small black berries. She never did get to see Tashmoo retrieve a duck, but we did learn that you could get poison ivy even in the winter.

One evening when Marlan was about seven-years-old I took her with me to the beach outside the Lagoon Pond drawbridge and set a fishing rod in a sand spike. We got into a silly argument and suddenly the rod arched over under the weight of a fish. By the time we could reach the rod the fish was gone.

I do not remember what we had argued about. But I do remember the line peeling off the reel and the excitement of losing a "big" fish.

On Monday Norma and I took Marlan to Vermont to begin her first year at college. When I returned to my desk late Monday  night the office was quiet and my attention fixed on a photo of Marlan taped to the side of my file cabinet.

She is holding a purple backpack. A paper name tag with her name, Marlan, is placed right next to the smiling daisy Norma had sewn onto the bib of her overalls in preparation for her first day of kindergarten at the Tisbury School. She has a bemused smile on her face, as if to say, "Dad, I'm fine. You can go now."

Monday morning in the Marlboro College parking lot, parents went through the transformative ritual of letting go of their children. Marlan, never one for ceremony, went through registration and then announced she was fine. "You can go now," she said. But one of the inescapable truths of being a dad is that your little girl grows up, and insists that she has grown up, but in your eyes she has never stopped being your little girl.

Monday night as I sat at my desk I looked at that photo and wiped off the dust that had accumulated over the years and cast into a sea of memories.

A Good Deed Is Returned During a Harrowing Offshore Trip

Paying it forward worked out well for one fortunate captain.
(July 2010)

FOR DAVE KADISON and Gary Mirando of Vineyard Haven, a pleasant day fishing well south of Martha's Vineyard for tuna and mahimahi turned into a frightening overnight return trip home, at the end of a Good Samaritan's tow rope amid crackling lightning bolts and heaving seas.

Cape-based charter captain and Massachusetts state trooper Terry Nugent drafted a gripping email account of the trip he titled, "Treat others as you would like to be treated."

Early Friday, Dave and Gary headed south aboard Poco Loco, Dave's 32-foot Mirage powerboat with a pilothouse and powered by a Volvo diesel outdrive. Their course was approximately 95 miles through the shipping lanes to an area known as Veatch Canyon. It was Gary's first offshore trip.

The men caught tuna and mahimahi. It was a great day of fishing. About 3 pm they headed back to the Vineyard. With about 60 miles between the boat and the Vineyard the transmission failed. They were dead in the water.

Dave called Sea Tow, a membership marine assistance service. The Sea Tow captain said the boat was beyond their range but that they would notify the Coast Guard.

The Coast Guard called Dave on his satellite phone to say they would assist if he were in imminent danger. The Coast Guard asked if there was anyone at sea nearby who might assist. Coincidently, charter captain Terry Nugent, aboard Riptide with two friends, was fishing in the same area.

Game plan change

In his email account, Captain Nugent said, "The game plan for the trip was to daytrip to Veatch Canyon for a shot at yellowfin, mahi and maybe a marlin ... All the safety gear was checked and rechecked like always, we never thought we would be needing it. We splashed the boat at 3 am in Falmouth, and in no time we were zipping along headed south."

They enjoyed a good day with plenty of action. Then, about 6 pm, "I pointed the big Contender north, and we were headed home at a nice smooth 40 mph," he wrote. "The idea of a cold drink and a nice long nap was running through my mind as I crossed into the shipping lanes about 70 miles from Wasque Point when the VHF crackled on 16."

Coast Guard calls even in an emergency are made in a distinct style and cadence: "PAN, PAN. Hello all stations, this is US Coast Guard Southeast New England — Break — The Coast Guard has received a call of a vessel disabled in the shipping lanes approximately 70 miles southeast of Martha's Vineyard. Any vessels in the area that are able to assist please contact United States Coast Guard Southeast New England."

Captain Nugent heard the Coast Guard hail Poco Loco and asked for their condition. He immediately recognized the name.

Captain Nugent continued, "I chimed in and Dave responded with a mix of anxiety and relief in his voice. Dave gave me his numbers, and he was about eight miles northwest of me. I advised the Coast Guard I was 10 minutes out from Poco Loco, and I told my crew, it's gonna be a long night.

Dave, an avid fisherman and swimming pool finisher, had good reason to be anxious. He was in the middle of the inbound shipping lanes. Earlier, he had watched on his radar as a large freighter 12 miles out followed a course straight for him. Frantic efforts to reach the ship's crew finally paid off, and the freighter changed course.

Terry arrived quickly in his 33-footer, powered by twin 275-horsepower Mercury engines. The men conferred on the best route home and then rigged a towline from Dave's anchor rope. Sea Tow planned to take over the tow when the boats reached Tom's Shoal off East Beach. The Coast Guard arranged to call and check their situation every hour.

The men had used Dave's satellite phone to relay messages to all their wives. Everybody's fine, we are just going to be a little late, was the message Dave said he relayed.

The seas were following and the wind was light from the southwest at 5 to 10 knots. It appeared it would be an easy trip. About three hours into the tow, the towing bridle snapped from the heaving of a larger than usual wave. The Coast Guard was advised, the vessels reconnected, and the men continued. The Coast Guard modified the communication schedule to every 30 minutes.

Prepare for worst

At 11:30 pm, the radio crackled with a Coast Guard broadcast: "PAN, PAN hello all stations. The Coast Guard has received a call from the National Weather Service that a strong line of severe thunderstorms is located between Martha's Vineyard and Block Island moving southeast at 35 knots. Strong rain, hail, and severe lightning are being accompanied by winds in excess of 35 knots. Break."

"Then they hailed us," Captain Nugent wrote. "This is not going to be good, I thought. They advised that the storms were headed right at us, and we should be prepared for the worst.

"They advised us to secure all hatches to avoid possible flooding from the torrential rains and to put on life vests. They went down a checklist of safety gear on both boats: rafts, flares, Gumby suits, etc. They put us on a 15-minute communication schedule.

"The next thirty minutes was calm but tense. We knew what was coming. I kicked the radar way out and then after a short time I saw the leading edge of the storm. It was heading right at us, and it was big. I advised the crew, and we all got ready for what was coming.

"Thirty minutes later the storm hit. The winds instantly went to 35 knots and the seas jumped to four to five feet making the already difficult tow infinitely harder. The rain came down like I've never seen before. My scuppers could barely keep up with the water flowing down the deck of the Riptide.

"We all huddled under the T-top for some level of shelter from the storm. The crew of Poco Loco was dry in the pilot house, but the unnatural motion of the tow, the heavy seas and the confined space of the pilot house gave them issues of their own. We pitched and heaved in the growing sea, and I tried to work the throttles as gently as I could to keep the strain even, as the boats tossed and turned independently of each other. In the big following seas Poco Loco would slide down a wave face and then heel over hard left or right when it got into the next wave.

"There was not enough keel to keep it straight under tow. Even my boat, which tracks like it's on rails, would heel over with the added strain of the tow. When they went in different directions, snap! Right in the middle of the storm we break the towline!

"With near zero visibility we tried to maneuver back to the Poco Loco. They hauled in the line to keep it out of our props, which would have been a nightmare. Dave made a great toss with the line and [a crew member] managed to catch the towline in the near zero visibility and stinging rain. We got the boat back in tow and advised the Coast Guard we were back under way. They put us on a ten-minute communication schedule."

Bad to worse

"That's when things went from bad to worse. Lightning! Big, bright and really, really close. We had all the riggers and rods down with nothing up but the VHF antenna so we could talk to the Coast Guard. The lightning had been in the distance, but that part of the storm was on us now, and the lightning was everywhere.

"As the lightning bolts hit closer and closer to us, I had to make a tough call. Antenna up for communications or down to avoid a lightning strike. I made the call to drop the antenna. Suddenly a few hundred yards away a blinding flash and an instant crack! The lightning hit the water only a few hundred feet away from us.

"I like to think that I'm calm and cool under pressure, but when a zillion watts of electricity hits that close and you're hanging onto a metal steering wheel, even the coolest hands get nervous.

"You just can't hide from lightning in the open ocean. Normally I can outrun storms or run hard to avoid or dodge them. But not tonight, not this time. The only way to run was to cut Poco Loco loose and set them adrift alone in the storm, and that wasn't happening. All we could do was pray that the gods had bad aim tonight."

Too close

On board the Poco Loco, Dave and Gary had broken out their red neoprene survival suits. They thought about putting them on but the suits were damp and moldy from storage. Instead, they stood on top of the suits hoping the insulation would shield them in the event of a strike.

"Absolutely, I was scared," Dave said. "We had one bolt that was right on top of us. It exploded like a flashbulb over our heads. It just made you shudder. Gary said, 'that was too close.'"

He knew that with only a T-top for protection, Terry was getting the worst of the storm.

"I kept telling him over the radio," Dave said, "you can cut us loose. Don't endanger your crew because of me. I can put out my sea anchor and wait for somebody else, and I have no problem with that."

Captain Nugent would not hear of the possibility. "I'm getting you in, I'm on a mission," he told Dave over the radio through the storm. The lightning quickly moved into the distance with the fast moving storm. The seas settled.

"Finally after three broken lines and nine hours of towing, we made it to Muskeget Channel," Captain Nugent wrote. "Dave called over the radio to give me the first good news of the night. Slack tide. We made it through the normally nasty piece of water without issue. The thought of the tow breaking and Poco Loco going aground on Wasque was one I had for the entire trip."

Poco Loco anchored up. Later that day, Sea Tow provided a tow back to Oak Bluffs.

Pay back

Captain Nugent said that during the 10-hour ordeal, he had a lot of time to think. "I thought about the times I've been towed in from various places over the years. One time in particular came to mind. About ten years ago, I was fishing in my bay boat off of Newport Rhode Island. The motor blew, and we were stranded 20 miles from the Westport River where we had launched.

"A guy in a big green custom center console came along and offered to help. I didn't know the guy, but he towed us for over two hours all the way back to the ramp at Westport. "When we got to the ramp I told the guy I didn't have much money on me, but I would send him whatever he wanted to cover the tow when I got home.

"The guy smiled and said, 'Don't worry about it. Maybe someday I'll be in a jam, and you can tow me home.' I told him I would if I ever got the chance. As the big green custom center console turned and headed out of the Westport River, I looked at the transom and said to myself, 'What a cool name for a boat, Poco Loco."

President Obama Needs to Take Time and Go Fishing

There is a lot to learn outside the Vineyard summer cocktail circuit. (August 2010)

THE POLITICAL PUNDITS will be lathered up this week. President Barack Obama and his family arrive on Martha's Vineyard for a summer vacation. I expect talk radio hosts will nip at this vacation like 3-D piranhas at the spring break float tube party scene from a cheap horror film. Critics will harp on the news that Michelle Obama did not buy her bathing suit at Walmart and the First Family rushed from the Gulf for the Vineyard — Chilmark no less.

Against the backdrop of a struggling economy, even the president's supporters wince a bit as they muster a half hearted defense: he needs to recharge (me too); he's not really on vacation even when he's on vacation (he needs to suck it up, he asked for the job); the president has a 24/7 job (like a Marine in Afghanistan doesn't?); he vacationed on the Island before he was president (not at exclusive Blue Heron Farm).

The critics think a vacation on Martha's Vineyard — toney, chic, elite, Hollywood-east, haven of the rich and powerful (take your pick of recent press adjectives) — shows the President is out of touch, that he just doesn't get it. There is some truth to that. But the inside-the-beltway group does not get it either. I want to help.

Although some visitors think they are elite, and that includes members of the press corps, it does not make all of the Vineyard elite. Eddy (Bonito Ed) Lepore, a retired tool engineer, and his wife Janet of Vernon, Connecticut spend each summer in the Martha's Vineyard Family Campground. They are not unlike other retired couples throughout the country, or the majority of people who call the Vineyard home.

At its heart, the Vineyard is about grabbing a fishing rod because the blues are at Wasque Rip, chasing blue claws in a salt pond or taking the long way around East Chop drive to take in the view of Nantucket Sound even if it takes a few extra minutes.

The last time Barack Obama visited the Vineyard he golfed at the Vineyard Golf Club, the same exclusive 18-hole course for members only in Edgartown course that Rush Limbaugh played on when he visited the Island. Ironic, huh?

I think it is time for the President to ditch the caddy shack look (even if Bill Murray, Vineyard summer resident, is a member of the same course) and forego socializing only with people he can hang out with in Washington. The President should go fishing.

Fishing is the great equalizer on Martha's Vineyard. It does not matter if you are staying in a rented room in Oak Bluffs or a Chilmark compound; there is the opportunity to have a great time casting under the stars from the beach at Wasque Rip or Lobsterville Beach.

During the derby — if you have to ask what that is you do not know as much as you think you know about Martha's Vineyard — venture capitalists fish and compete with Island carpenters. And the fish do not care who you are.

More than 48 million people in this country fish. They fish from the shore, they fish from all manner of boat: Wooden skiffs on lakes, bass boats outfitted to look like a NASCAR racecar that go almost as fast, and sportfishermen that are as luxuriously outfitted as a Miami condo.

According to "Fisheries Economics of the United States 2006," a NOAA report that covers 1997 to 2006, recreational fishing generated $82 billion in sales, $24 billion in income, and supported 534,000 jobs in 2006.

On Martha's Vineyard fishermen support businesses with names like Coop's, Larry's, Dick's, and Porky's. These are businesses that pay taxes and hire local people who spend money in our community and help out folks when they are down on their luck in many little ways that never make the news.

Cooper Gilkes, owner of Coop's and my friend, is a hunter and a fisherman. He doesn't golf and he is not chic, but he does know how to fish.

The President could learn a lot from Coop about fishing, the Vineyard, and what concerns the country. Coop and his wife Lela, a person who embodies the qualities of fairness and generosity of spirit much of the world associates with the United States, built a successful business out of their house. Lela does the books. She knows how much of her family's income from all those plugs, rods and reels goes to the government.

I recently read a story in the New York Times, "Pakistani taxes widen divide between rich and poor," that reported that even as we send that country billions of our tax dollars in aid, out of more than 170 million Pakistanis, fewer than 2 percent pay income tax, and most of the very rich pay nothing at all.

Maybe the President could stop in at Coop's and explain to Cooper and Lela why they are asked to share their hard-earned tax dollars with Pakistan when that country's elite do not.

Every winter Island tackle shop owners such as Steve Purcell at Larry's order from shops around the country; that keeps other people working. If Steve misjudges there is no multi-million dollar payday on the way out the door. No bailout. Closed. Down with the ship.

Tackle shops do not sell derivatives. They sell eels, squid, line, and hooks and dispense fishing advice. Small shops like Dick's rely on their hard-won reputations for honest dealings and personal service. Maybe you could stop in and talk to Stevie Morris, owner of the shop named after his grandfather. You probably saw it on your way to lunch with your pal and advisor, Valerie Jarrett in Oak Bluffs.

I do not want to play the role of presidential advisor and critic Dick Morris but far more people could relate to a photo of the President taking a scup off the hook than swinging at a golf ball at a private club with a $300,000 membership fee, or playing hoops at a vacation home that rents for $25,000 a week.

Martha's Vineyard is a very good choice for a vacation if you want to fish. There is nothing fancy about catching scup from Memorial Wharf or bottom fishing from a skiff in Vineyard Sound, or sitting on an upturned bucket next to Janet Messineo bait fishing for striped bass.

How misguided are the reporters parroting back knocks on the Vineyard? Well, the Washington Post, which should know a thing or two about the Vineyard given the ties between the Graham family, owners of the newspaper and West Tisbury, recently published a piece titled, "Why vacation, Obamas, when you could have a great staycation here in D.C.?"

The story, written by writers who I assume are irritated that they are stuck in the city in August, described all the wonderful activities Washington has to offer. This one caught my eye.

"What does Maryland have that Martha's Vineyard doesn't? Steamed blue crabs. For great crustaceans and a waterfront view, the Obamas should head for Mike's Crab House, just outside Annapolis, where diners sit outdoors at picnic tables enjoying a feast — $65 for a dozen large crabs — with all the fixins while watching boats drift by."

No blue claws on Martha's Vineyard? I have news for President Obama — don't believe everything you read about Martha's

Vineyard. On Sunday I joined a crabbin' expedition that included Coop, Ned Casey, and two guys who have never had to chase their food — fellow New Yorkers and longtime seasonal Island visitors Barry Adams of Oak Bluffs and Andy Peterson of Vineyard Haven.

Catching crabs is about simple fun. All you need a long-handled crab net and floating tub or bucket. I recommend polarized sunglasses and solid footwear in the event you step on a crab and it objects.

Barry Adams (left) and Andy Peterson display a barrel
of blue crabs netted in Edgartown Great Pond.

Sometimes you see the crab, and sometimes the crab sees you. The little crustaceans swim fast. You need to be quick. Steam them up as you would a lobster. There is nothing toney about eating fresh-caught steamed Island blue claw crabs on an outdoor deck. Just dig in and get messy.

President Obama and his girls would have a great time netting blue claws just steps from his back door on Tisbury Great Pond. I would be happy to assist.

Manhood Is On the Line When the Squid are Running

A wife casts doubt on her husband's ability to perform.
(June 2011)

THE COWBOY IS towing a horse trailer up a dirt road. His truck gets stuck in the mud. The denim clad guy gets out and hitches the horses to the truck. In a sonorous voice the narrator says, "This is the age of knowing how to make things happen."

The not-so-subliminal message is that a real man does not let a problem keep him down. The commercial was all about being a macho man. It was not to sell trucks, but Viagra.

All men want to perform. Sunday of last week, I did not feel like a real man. I did not need Viagra. I needed a pink squid jig.

Last year about this time, I introduced my wife Norma to the fun of jigging for squid off the beach (that is not a metaphor — I really mean jigging for squid). It was so much fun that when I suggested we grab a pizza from Giordano's and go to State Beach before sunset to jig for squid she thought it was a great idea.

Squid jigs have inverted wire tines in place of the hooks one normally associates with fishing lures. In their non-fried calamari state, squid are aggressive predators. They move quite quickly and grab prey with their tentacles.

When a squid grabs a jig, the fisherman, if he is quick, gives a quick tug and impales the tentacles on the tines. Often, in its efforts to escape, the squid will move through a series of pulsating color changes — white, red, brown — and squirt water and ink.

For that reason, it is a good reason to go squidding in the clothes you would wear to clean your basement or attic. Many an inquisitive well-dressed Edgartown visitor has wandered too close to a Memorial Wharf squidder to take a look at what is going on and received a well-timed squirt of ink, much to the delight of any local kids.

You might not think so, but squid jigs come in all shapes, sizes and colors. There are the small jigs weighing less than one-ounce used by Island squidders, and the "Giant Humboldt" ten-inch, 15-ounce squid jigs used in Puget Sound.

I am not very good at catching squid. I am not a "squid whisperer" like my friends Coop or Tom. I go when the occasion presents and I catch squid for fluke bait. On that particular day, I grabbed a light freshwater rod and my only two squid jigs, one yellow and one white. Norma and I stopped for pizza and headed to the picnic tables on State Beach.

There were about five guys on the beach casting squid jigs. We had not expected to find clouds of biting gnats. We enjoyed our pizza in the truck.

I walked down to the beach while Norma remained behind in the bug-free comfort of the car. I tossed my jig out and felt a subtle grab, but the squid retreated.

Squid will sometimes attack a jig; or, they will timidly swim up to it, take a quick look, maybe even reach out for a touch and retreat.

I could not catch a squid — not one. For 20 minutes I cast and retrieved, cast and retrieved. I would groan every time I thought I had one and lost it. The guys next to me were hauling squid in, one after another.

"It's gotta be pink," a sympathetic squidder said to me.

I kept at it without success. I varied my retrieve. I cursed and cajoled. I tried to pretend it was not happening but it was.

"How's it going honey?" Norma said after emerging from the car.

"Not so good," I said. "I can't catch a goddamn squid."

The guys next to me continued to drag squirting squid out of the water. If it had been humiliating before, it was doubly humiliating with my wife standing next to me and observing my pain with some degree of glee. I was determined to catch at least one squid.

I said that one of the squidders had volunteered that pink was the hot color. "They will only hit pink," I said.

"Don't you have a pink squid?" Norma asked.

"No, I don't."

"Why not?" she said. "When we went with Coop last year he had a whole box of jigs."

"Well, I don't," I said.

I continued to cast; and cast; and cast. "Let's go," I finally said.

On the ride home Norma was sympathetic to a degree. I thought to myself, this is the age of knowing how to make things happen.

On Monday, I returned to the beach with a pink squid jig. I caught a squid my first cast. Dennis Gough of New York state who had stood next to me the night before was back again for more squid. He and his fishing pals would catch just what they needed to go fishing that evening.

Reflecting on my previous ordeal, Dennis was sympathetic. "I hate when that happens," he said.

I could not agree more.

Fishermen's Bonds Were
Forged in Combat

For Joe Lopez, an unexpected trip to Martha's Vineyard was the setting for an extraordinary reunion with a man he had never met. (October 2014)

THE MARTHA'S VINEYARD Striped Bass and Bluefish Derby ended last week in a frenzy of activity. Amid all the excitement it would have been easy to overlook a small group of Island visitors, veterans of combat, some of whom were still recovering from grievous wounds suffered in Afghanistan, They stayed on the Island from Sunday to Thursday where they enjoyed fishing and the hospitality extended to them by the Nixon family of Chilmark, and a group of dedicated Island volunteers.

Five years ago on October 3, 2009, Army First Sergeant Jonathan Hill woke up to the sound of gunfire and rocket explosions when up to 400 Taliban attacked 53 U.S. soldiers based in Combat Outpost (COP) Keating set at the bottom of three steep mountains just 14 miles from the Pakistan border. Retired after 21 years in service to his country, last week Jon's only concern was how to improve his luck after being out-fished by retired Marine Joe Roberts, who despite his wheelchair and falling over at least once, kept catching all the fish while out with Island charter captain Scott McDowell, one of a group of Menemsha captains who donated their time and boats in a community-based effort known as the the American Heroes Saltwater Challenge.

Now in its sixth year, the fishing respite began when Jack Nixon, then 7, saw a newspaper photo essay about the challenges facing Iraq and Afghanistan veterans, and told his dad, Bob Nixon, a documentary filmmaker, that he wished some veterans could fish the derby.

Jake Tapper, CNN anchor and chief Washington correspondent, described COP Keating, the men and their battle in his best-selling book, "The Outpost: An Untold Story of American Valor," published by Little, Brown and Company. The daylong battle left eight American soldiers dead and twenty-two more wounded, making it one of the deadliest military fights in decades.

Mr. Tapper and his wife are friends of Bob and Sarah Nixon, owners of the Beach Plum Inn, Menemsha Inn, and Home Port restaurant. One year earlier, Ms. Nixon called Mr. Tapper to see who among the group of men he had chronicled might like to visit the Island and participate in the Saltwater Challenge. It was the start of a new chapter that placed COP Keating at the nucleus of the Island event.

COP Keating, which was slated to be closed, came under attack from all sides just before 6 am. The attackers quickly overran the base and within the first hour, the American defenders had "collapsed their perimeter" to the immediate area around the command post, which became "their final fighting position."

At the Beach Plum Inn during a break in the fishing, golfing, and eating schedule, Jon Hill spoke about what it meant to serve his country, the Army, the men he served with, and his work as a member of the board of directors of the Defenders of Freedom, a group that assists active and retired military members.

"I'll tell you, those were some of the best men that the United States Army ever had in one spot, in one fight and I couldn't be prouder of the guys I served with," Sergeant Hill said. "The men there fought valiantly, they fought hard and they did some phenomenal things under the worst circumstances."

Medically retired, Jon, 42, lives in Louisiana with his wife and two children, a 13-year-old girl and a boy, 17. He said what he misses most about the Army is being with young soldiers, watching them grow, mentoring them, "and putting them on a good path to success."

Jake Tapper called and told him about the Vineyard trip. "I was not going to say no," he said. "It's a once in a lifetime chance for folks like me."

There was one regret. "I really wished I could bring my family," he said. "There are a lot of spouses and children that go through a lot of pain while their loved ones are deployed and I think they should get recognized a little more than they do."

Jon likes to fish and hunt. But most of his time is spent working on behalf of Defenders of Freedom. "The best therapy for me is helping other vets move forward," he said. The organization offers a menu of services to help veterans who are making the transition from military to civilian life get back on their feet. "Being in military is like being institutionalized, you get so used to doing things so differently from the civilian world," he said.

Across the dining room, West Point graduate Captain Rahul Harpalani was having a grand time with his fellow fishermen. Next year he will leave the military and enter Columbia Business School. Sergeant Hill and Capt. Harpalani first met at COP Keating. On May 15, 2010, Lieutenant Harpalani lost his leg to an IED (improvised explosive device).

"What makes me so proud to know him and say I would follow a guy like that into hell," Jon said, "is he is a torch-bearing leader. He is an example of the ethos of, I will never quit. He has moved forward, he has rehabilitated himself, and now he is a captain in the Army and when he was injured he was a lieutenant. He is a testament to the fact that you can continue to move forward and continue to do great things and I have a lot of respect for that. He is setting a huge example."

Jon said he was asleep when the attack on COP Keating occurred. He and the other members of his platoon had no time to don body armor. "It was just chaos outside," he said. His first concern was getting men and ammo to guard positions.

What Jon never mentioned as we spoke was the Silver Star he received "for exceptional valor in action against an armed enemy." The citation states that Sergeant First Class Hill "led and directed his platoon while exposing himself to a heavy barrage of enemy fire. With no regard for his own personal safety, Sergeant First Class Hill organized multiple efforts to recover fallen soldiers under effective, accurate fire."

The full citation only hints at the drama of the battle and the selfless nature of ordinary men caught in an extraordinary situation. That day was far from his mind last Tuesday. "I've had the best two days I've had in a long time, catching fish or not," Jon Hill told me. Before he would leave the Vineyard, Jon would also would make a difference in the life of one soldier still grappling with the loss of a brother in arms and create another link in a story now intertwined with the derby and the Vineyard.

Joseneth (Joe) Lopez, Army specialist 1st Infantry Division, was stationed at COP Keating in 2008. After 12 months of intermittent fire and just three months prior to the battle, Joe's unit was transferred out. Specialist Nathan Nash, a senior member of the same platoon, remained behind a few weeks to help introduce the new men to the surrounding area. The newcomers to COP Keating included Sergeant Hill, who by coincidence had been Nathan's drill sergeant in basic training.

One of the men newly assigned to COP Keating was Stephen Mace, Joe's bunkmate and best friend throughout basic training. The two men, one arriving and the other departing, reconnected briefly at COP Keating. Months later Joe learned his friend Stephen Mace was among the battle dead.

Joe, 25, left the military and moved to Orlando to attend school, but the memory of his best friend's death in a base he had left continued to haunt him. Last fall, Nathan Nash was a member of the group of soldiers that visited the Vineyard and he encouraged Joe to make the Vineyard trip this year and speak to Jon Hill.

Last week, with Menemsha as a backdrop Jon Hill and Joe Lopez met for the first time. "We sat down and we spoke and I told him about Mace and he told me he was his platoon sergeant and he told me how he passed away and I finally got closure out of it due to this magical trip," Joe told me in a phone call Tuesday. "We were able to hug it out and I felt like for a second that Mace was next to me and at that point it was beautiful."

They spoke about Mace and how great a person he was and how he lives through them. Joe said that he had not been able to stop mourning his lost friends. The Vineyard embrace, the beauty of the environment, "no sense of rush or regular life," helped soothe his pain.

"A lot of questions were put to rest because of First Sergeant Hill and the way he was able to close those wounds," Joe said. "It's crazy. We don't know each other from nowhere, but somehow the stars align and we all got to talk about it." On Martha's Vineyard.

Has Martha's Vineyard
Gone to the Dogs?

In the Baskerville section of Edgartown, a wealthy property owner threatens to release the hounds on trespassers.
(July 2015)

THERE ARE MANY things to consider when heading out to fish the Martha's Vineyard shoreline. The tide, wind direction, any concentrations and type of bait, and ease of access come immediately to mind. Guard dogs do not.

This week, The Times received a Letter to the Editor from Mary Marro of Oak Bluffs, who said she had been walking along the Edgartown shoreline with a fishing rod when she encountered a sign that warned of video surveillance and guard dogs. "What kind of landowner would post this?" she asked.

It is a good question. I would understand a sign that read, "This beach patrolled by deer ticks" ... or greenheads, or saltwater mosquitoes, but guard dogs? This is Martha's Vineyard, not Detroit or the Hamptons. I decided to investigate.

Late Friday morning, I parked at Bend-in-the-Road. I grabbed my eight-foot St. Croix rod, tied on a bubble-gum-colored Sluggo and stuck some dog biscuits in my pocket, and began walking along the beach that borders Cow Bay.

I quickly left behind the smell of humans basted in tanning lotion and walked past rows of wooden cabanas along Cow Bay. Further up the beach I saw a man in a bright yellow T shirt. There was a sign on a post in the sand. To my relief, the man in the shirt was not holding a version of horror novelist Stephen King's Cujo on a leash.

As I approached, the young man walked in my direction. His T-shirt said "security" on it in bold letters. He greeted me very pleasantly and said the beach was private property and that if I wanted to keep walking he could not stop me, but would I please respect the privacy of the owners. And he asked to see my fishing license.

I told him I appreciated the fact that he was only doing his job, but that I was not going to show him my fishing license; that I was well aware of my right to fish along that stretch of shore in or out of the water below the high-water mark; and I planned to write about this little corner of the world.

The young man, an Islander, said he also liked to fish and hunt. He explained that strollers carrying useless equipment sometimes used the excuse of fishing to gain access to what was a private beach. The owners, he said, only wanted people to respect their privacy, "just as anyone would."

I will give the young man credit. He was polite and well-spoken. He said he recently had to ask two women carrying useless Zebco rods not to trespass. He said, "You looked like you knew what you were doing."

I explained that if I had seen terns diving off bait in front of the beach, I would have headed right for the birds, but as I was only interested in checking out the sign, I was content to leave it at that and had no interest that day in walking further.

"No trespassing. This property is protected by video surveillance. Trespassers will be prosecuted," read one sign with an image of a camera for effect. And in case you did not get the message, another sign under that one said, "No trespassing. Guard dogs on duty."

Shoreline access is a contentious issue around the country. People like to walk along the ocean. On the other hand, property owners who shell out millions of dollars for waterfront property and pay huge annual tax bills expect some degree of privacy along with their assessment.

Massachusetts is one of several states that grant ownership to the low-water mark. The colonial ordinances commonly come up in any debate over access to the Island shoreline.

They were enacted between 1641 and 1647 by the Great and General Court, the term now applied to the state legislature. At that time, Massachusetts gave property owners property rights to the mean low-water mark. The intent was to stimulate the building of piers, wharves, and shoreside commerce. But the colonial government retained the rights for the public along the tidelands to "fishing, fowling, and navigating."

"Everie inhabitant who is an hous-holder thall have free fishing and fowling, in any great Ponds, Bayes, Coves and Rivers so far as the Sea ebs and flows, within the precincts of the town where they dwell, unless the free-men of the same town, or the General Court have otherwise appropriated them ..."

"... It is declared that in all creeks, coves and other places, about and upon salt water where the sea ebbs and flows, the Proprietor of the land adjoyning shall have proprietie to the low water mark where the sea doth not ebb above a hundred rods, and not more whereforever it ebbs farther. Provided that such Proprietor shall not by this libertie have power to stop or hinder the passage of boats or other vessels in, or through any sea creeks, or coves to other mens houses or lands."

Some time back, when writing about this same topic, I spoke to David Hoover, general counsel for the Division of Fisheries and Wildlife and Environmental Law Enforcement. Mr. Hoover told me, "Assuming a person arrives at the tidelands legally, they may fish, fowl, or navigate, but must still obey local laws and not damage property or interfere with the property owners' enjoyment of their property."

It all comes down to common sense and consideration. Packing a picnic basket and carrying a broken fishing rod does not meet the test. Whooping and hollering at 1 am over a big fish is not a considerate exercise of the rights guaranteed in the colonial ordinance.

A check of town assessor records showed the $9 million Cow Bay property is owned by limited liability companies based in Greenwich, Conn. A few phone calls led me to the name of the owner, C. Dean Metropoulos, a self-made investor who is a testament to the American success story. According to Forbes magazine, Mr. Metropoulos is worth $2.1 billion, which buys a lot of sand.

Mr. Metropoulos and his sons Evan and Daren take beaten-down brands and spruce them up, according to Forbes. They sold Pabst Brewing in 2014 for an estimated $750 million, three times what they paid for the company in 2011. Their next fixer-upper is Hostess Brands, which they bought out of bankruptcy with Apollo Global Management in 2013.

From what I could learn from Bass and Bluefish Derby records, Evan is the fisherman in the family. In 2010, he weighed in a 31.25-pound striped bass in the boat division that temporarily held the first-place spot. That may have been the year the family hired a Menemsha charter captain for the entirety of the derby.

There are a few property owners who employ beach security guards to keep wandering plebeians — How do you tell a plebeian from a patrician in a Speedo? Plebeians don't wear Speedos — off generally deserted stretches of beach, but I do not think there is another sign on the Island that references guard dogs. How would that look in one of the magazines devoted to telling the rest of the world how "special" the Vineyard is?

I tried unsuccessfully to reach Evan Metropoulos to see if he would mount the "Twinkie defense." Maybe he put the sign up after eating too many Twinkies washed down with too many Blue Ribbons.

The family has been visiting Martha's Vineyard for years. One would think some of the Island's charm and sensibility would have rubbed off on them. To paraphrase Ronald Reagan: Mr. Metropoulos, take down that sign.

Chummers and Anglers at the Old Bass Stand

Squibnocket Point, once home to the fabled Squibnocket Club, continues to attract fishermen.

FISHING HAS ITS temples: spots of rock, sand and surging water with a special presence and atmosphere that link us with fishing's history, traditions, and the lore of fishermen long since gone.

More than one hundred years ago, striped bass clubs organized by some of America's most prominent men came into existence. They were places of rural comfort where the affairs of the country were discussed on an equal footing with the size of that day's catch, and eating and drinking was serious business. The island of Cuttyhunk, at the west end of the Elizabeth Islands and Squibnocket Point, on the southwest corner of Martha's Vineyard, were two of the better-known locations.

Both of these clubs flourished during the period following the Civil War before fading into fishing history behind a decline in the numbers of fish that had inspired their existence. The Cuttyhunk club house is now a private residence [Since turned into a bed and breakfast], and the Squibnocket club house, partially a victim of fire and erosion, was eventually moved to another island location for use as a barn. However, both names still evoke a sense of reverence in traditional surf fishermen. And, though the clubs may be gone and much of the surrounding property is private, as the century ends conservation measures have returned the striped bass to the waters these grand club houses once overlooked.

The Squibnocket Club was formed in 1869. And according to the notes of the late Dr. John Cunningham of Boston, the club house was a substantial building on a high cliff with a large living room, many bedrooms and a large porch where members could sit and watch the fishing action on the eight different bass stands, including one conveniently connected directly to the porch. Up to one hundred feet in length, the stands were narrow wooden walkways constructed of spruce, which was less slippery when wet than pine, and supported by iron rods driven into the boulders that extended out over the water. At the end of each was a wooden seat where the intrepid angler, usually dressed in coat and tie, would sit.

It is certain that the five-foot, copper striped bass weather-vane atop the Squibnocket Club must have been a welcome and inspiring sight to the weary angler coming from Boston or New York in the late 1800's. Today, a trip from the ferry port of Vineyard Haven takes approximately twenty-five minutes by car, but when the Vineyard was a quieter and less developed island the approximately 22 mile trip on sandy country roads required a half day journey by carriage.

Captain Hartson H. Bodfish, a native Vineyarder and whaling captain, wrote in his book, "Chasing The Bowhead," about his days as a young man with a summer job driving carriages. He relates, "Twelve members, all men of wealth, had established this club and equipped the place for catching striped bass with rod and reel. Long walks of plank ran out over the rocks, secured by means of irons set in drill holes in the boulders. And from the ends of these walks or stands the fishermen would cast into the surf for bass.

"There were some national celebrities among the men who came to catch bass. Elihu Root, New York senator, statesman and Nobel Peace Prize winner, for example, ex-President Chester

Arthur, Dr. Louis Agassiz, naturalist and founder of the Harvard Museum of Comparative Zoology and many others. Most of them were fine people, but there were some that I grew to dislike, particularly the children, who wanted to stop and pick all the wildflowers, thus delaying us on the way. Besides taking these people to the clubhouse, I carted tons and tons of bass to the boat, for these sportsmen wanted to take their trophies home with them or ship them to friends."

Captain Bodfish would probably be no less enamored with some of the children of today's wealthy summer visitors to the Vineyard, but then, as now, the rigors of the seasonal Island economy brought locals and the famous together. One of the more interesting relationships was that of the fisherman and his "chummer." Usually a local, the chummer procured the bait, set up a chum slick to attract the bass, and often gaffed the fish from the rocks beneath the stand.

It was a position of some importance and one that engendered a great deal of mutual respect. Chum slicks were generally started using a mixture of chopped-up menhaden, and lobster bodies and claws. The lobster tail was saved to bait the hook. This may seem extravagant by today's lobster prices, but then you need to consider that these wealthy anglers were paying approximately $1.50 per hundred lobsters.

When we think of these well-to-do anglers who neither baited their own hooks, gaffed their own fish or generally even carried them back to the club it would be easy to assume that they lacked a certain fisherman's edge and toughness that today's hard core surf fishermen take pride in. But make no mistake about it. These men may have lived the good life but they were striper fishermen to the bone with a determination that any modern day striper enthusiast would respect.

Francis Endicott, a 19th century writer and fisherman, wrote about a number of the bass clubs of his day and in one passage related the story of Seth Green, a member of the Cuttyhunk club, who was held in great respect both by the chummers and fishermen of his era. Mr. Endicott refers to him as the "great father of fishes" because as a New York State superintendent he was responsible for some of the first fish stocking programs throughout the state.

On a particularly rough day, but "when the bass were biting freely," Seth Green found himself caught in a huge wave breaking over the stand he was fishing on. Completely drenched, he left the stand only to return carrying a rope and "in spite of the warnings and remonstrances of his friends," tied himself to the seat. Then, with waves continuing to break over the stand, Seth Green continued to fish.

This story was related to Mr. Endicott by one of the Cuttyhunk club chummers and he mentions that the "pluck of the old man" elicited the chummer's admiration in a way "which no amount of piscicultural skill could have commanded." And it is a tale that even today would be approved of knowingly by any striper fisherman from Montauk to Nantucket.

In club days the goal was to hold the honor of "high hook," the fisherman who had caught the heaviest striper, and records that tell of fifty and sixty pounders caught on wooden rods with "thumb-stall" drags reflect the skill of the fishermen. The Cutty Hunk Club high-hook in 1882 was W.R. Renwick with a 64 pound striper. And in 1878, F.O. Herring claimed high-hook honors at the Pasque Island Club with a 60.5 pound bass.

According to the Squibnocket Club fish log, the fishing was best in the club's first year - 1869 - when 620 stripers weighing a total of 5,040 pounds were weighed in. The average weight was eight pounds with the largest tipping the scales at 54 pounds. And the largest bass ever weighed in on the club scales was a fifty-eight pounder landed by A. Greene on June 19, 1873. However, by 1888 only 13 fish were taken with an average weight of 16 pounds.

Fishermen still fish the waters of the Squibnocket Bass club by driving to Squibnocket town beach in the town of Chilmark. There is a "residents only" parking lot, but in the off-season or during the early morning or at night they are free to park and make the arduous long hike along the rocky shore to the point where the old bass stands stood. If there's enough light and they have a discerning eye they can spot some of the old drilled holes and know they are fishing in the footsteps of some great Americans.

For anyone who decides to cast a plug to the striped bass that once again swim in the breaking surf and surging currents of Squibnocket, now, as in the past, Francis Endicott's admonition for would-be striper fishermen will stand true; that, unless you can "take a thorough soaking philosophically and as a matter of course, you had better give up all thought of being a bass fisherman."

Derby Madness

Nelson Sigelman holds a 31.29 pound striped bass he caught to win the fly rod shore division in the 1996 Martha's Vineyard Striped Bass and Bluefish Derby.

I started to worry when I had the dream. I'm not sure where I was, but all of a sudden big bluefish — derby size winners — were swimming by me in a narrow sluiceway. I couldn't believe it! Finally, after weeks of no success, I had a chance to catch a big blue from the shore on my fly rod. I cast and dropped a fly right in front of one of the fish. Details are hazy after that, but when I got the fish to shore, it was already gutted. I couldn't weigh it in! I had hooked a zombie bluefish! Night of the Living Dead bluefish!

I was worried about what the dream said about my mental state until I walked into Coop's tackle shop in Edgartown. I started telling Coop about my dream when another fisherman in the shop said that he'd been having fishing dreams too, except in his most recent dream he was catching white poodles!

Now, that's weird, I thought, feeling better about myself. Hell, at least in my dream I was catching fish.

Why She Hates the Bass
and Bluefish Derby

Fishing is relaxing? Not the way we do it.
(October 1994)

THE DERBY ENDED just in time to save my marriage. I knew that when I came home and found my wife Norma had started a list that read: The Top Ten Reasons Why I Hate the Derby. The first on the list: "My husband becomes even more of a selfish, insensitive monster than usual ..." It was obvious my fishing habits had taken their toll on even my wife's apparently unlimited patience.

And how could I argue? I would return home from fishing exhausted and, like the victim of some rare tropical fever speaking in a delirium, I would babble about where the fish were, where they might be, and when they might be there before dropping into sleep. I was a victim of a uniquely Vineyard disease, called "derby madness." Its symptoms appear each year as September gives way to October and it casts its spell over even the most casual of fishermen.

Early symptoms include: the voluntary cleaning and arranging of all fishing rods, lures, reels and paraphernalia that has been one massive entangled mess all summer; an unsolicited invitation from one's spouse to go out for dinner (a sure sign of ulterior motives); and a return from the local tackle shop carrying unmarked brown bags.

As the derby proceeds and the symptoms become all too apparent it is important to recognize some of the advanced stages of derby madness in those you care about. Otherwise you may feel that someone you care about is exhibiting signs of a truly disturbed personality. And actually they are. But it tends to end at the last ring of the weigh station bell unless they've always been like that. Every year you tell yourself that this derby will be different and every year it's the same.

As I had for many years, I took the last week of the derby off from work so I could concentrate on fishing. It is a tradition grounded in the reality that in the final weeks of the derby I throw off any pretense of thinking about anything else but fish. This focus may be hard for some to understand, but there is something intoxicating in a single-minded pursuit even when it concerns fish and, as the last weigh-in draws closer, every angler believes he or she is only one cast away from a derby winner.

Early in the week Gary Look of Edgartown caught a 12.44 pound bonito on spinning gear from his boat off Cape Poge light to set a new derby record and win the Grand Prize. And on the last day I caught a 10.81-pound bonito on my fly rod.

My fish would turn out to take first place in the boat bonito fly rod category — my first winning fish in any derby — and set a new fly rod record. But the best prize of all came in the form of a card, written by my three-and-a-half- year- old daughter, and guided by my wife's hand, that read, "Daddy, I'm so proud of you for catching the big one. Love, Marlan."

The derby was over and I was reminded of a conversation I had when I picked up a hitchhiker. He noticed the fishing gear in the car and commented that,

"Oh, you like to fish. That must be very relaxing."

I just laughed, turned to him and said, "Not the way we do it."

Desperate Columnist Asks the Gypsy for an Edge

A fisherman seeks to recover his derby mojo.
(October 1999)

I NEEDED HELP. I needed guidance. It was halfway through the derby and I hadn't caught a fish big enough to bring to the weigh station.

It was time to put the tide chart aside, stop discussing the fortunes of fishing with the tackle shop gurus, and seek professional help. I decided to consult Duchess, a self-described Gypsy fortune teller, at her home and office on New York Avenue in Oak Bluffs. Maybe, I thought, she could use her skills to point me in the right direction.

It happens every derby. For some fishermen, everything swims their way. Sure, skill and effort plays a big part, but there is also something I call "derby mojo." In this derby, so far, I had no derby mojo.

Scott Patterson had it in a big way. Two days in a row he had caught first place false albacore in a sea of small fish. Stan Popowitz had it too. For the second year in a row, the heaviest shore bonito had found his hook.

Kevin Honan, casting to fish at 3 am in the morning at Cape Poge gut watched his truck roll off the bank and stop, up to the front windshield, in the channel. He didn't have derby mojo.

Duchess greeted me at the door apologizing for a cold she said she had picked up on a recent visit to New York City. Wearing a plain black dress but no hoop earrings, she invited me to sit at a small round table in her living room and make myself comfortable. A deck of cards was placed in the center of the table. On the wall behind me was a picture of President Abraham Lincoln.

I wondered if there was some special connection between Mr. Lincoln and Gypsy culture. Later, I learned the answer was interior design — Duchess liked the antique feel of the black and white photo.

I told Duchess that I was fishing in the derby, a large Island fishing tournament. Not wanting to be rude but getting straight to the point, I leaned forward and told her I wasn't really interested in my general fortune.

"You know," I said, "I'm most interested in my specific fishing fortune over the next two weeks."

I added that if her powers could be extended, I'd appreciate some suggestions about where to fish.

Duchess smiled kindly. She explained that cards and lines in a palm were only a conduit. They would be used, she said, "to tune into my vibrations."

Obviously sensitive to any negative comparisons, she said the "new psychics of today" had made the art of fortune telling into a "carnival." Anyone, she explained, could take a pack of Tarot cards and read the backs for a fortune that might by coincidence hit the mark. She had a "gift," that is the birthright of Gypsy women, she said.

Slightly embarrassed, I did not mention that a few years ago, in the interests of research, I called La Toya Jackson's psychic hotline to ask when the first bonito would be caught on the Vineyard.

"So," I said, impressed by her sincerity, "by coming here I'm getting the real thing?"

"Exactly," Duchess said with a hint of pride.

"But what about credentials," I asked?

She explained, "It's been going on for generations and generations, since the world began. Only Gypsies have been giving out readings, long ago called fortune telling."

"That's pretty good for me then," I said, delivering a vote of confidence.

"Each and every one of us is psychic in some ways," Duchess said, "but it is a gift given to Gypsy women."

The bass fishing is usually poor during a full moon, but I still wanted to be able to fish without getting down on four legs. Mindful of people who anger Gypsies in the movies, I had to ask a question.

"If I write something you don't like," I asked Duchess, "are you going to put a curse on me?"

"I don't believe in curses. I believe in creating your own curse," she said.

It was clear to me I had created my own derby curse. I told her I needed some guidance.

"I'll give it a shot," she said with a smile. She asked me to hold out my hand.

With a glance at the lines in my palm, Duchess looked me in the eyes as her voice took on a rhythmic, melodious tone.

"I will tell you the past, I will tell you some of the present, and I will tell you what is now. Deep inside the future I will not go, but I will point it out to you."

This was sounding good. It had a better feel than Coop telling me he thought there might be some fish around Cape Poge because the bait was packing in.

Duchess continued, describing my personality and my deepest thoughts. She mixed all that with some power of positive thinking suggestions. She advised me to think "positively and remove confusion from your mind."

"When you don't know where you stand," she said, "you could easily lose the shoes from your feet and you don't even know they're gone."

But catching fish, not personal growth, was really my interest. Breaking into her discourse, I asked, "But are you able to get some sense whether my fishing luck will change in the next two weeks?"

In patient tones she said, "I told you there are no curses. People create their own curses. See, that's what I believe. Now, in luck it is what you are going to make your luck to be."

I could not just expect God to drop a fish on me. She told me I would have to fish hard to catch a fish. I couldn't argue with that. Most of the current derby leaders had not moved from their fishing spots.

"In other words," she said, "get out and do it."

Still, I needed an edge. I spread out a map of the Island on the table. "Is there any place you might get a sense about where I should go?" I asked.

"You have to struggle a little," she told me.

"I'd like to cut down on the struggle part," I answered.

Intent on returning to my personal growth, she posed a question: "When you are out there, you really don't challenge those people you are competing with. When you are out there, who do you challenge?"

She paused like a teacher waiting for a student to give an obvious answer. She asked again, "Who do you challenge?"

"Myself," I said obligingly.

"Exactly!" she said, pleased with my correct response.

But I moved us back to the issue at hand. She looked away from the map and told me "she will give me two choices without looking." Her finger moved slowly over the map.

"Here," she said, and "here." I mark both spots with a pen. Both are places I have caught fish before, I told Duchess.

"I'm not going to tell you I'm right about or I'm wrong about this, but I am a Gypsy that goes by my feelings. We trust our feelings, we live by our feelings," she said.

I am picturing myself with a derby winner already. I try to bring it into focus. Pointing to a picture of the four derby fish, I ask her which fish I should concentrate my efforts to catch.

Holding up her finger, she told me, "This is not your choice, it's their choice to come to you. If it were your choice, you could hand pick any one."

She reassured me, "Lets just say you're going to go out there and give it your best shot. Let's say you don't catch fish, you are still a winner because you tried."

Before I departed I asked Duchess if any other derby fishermen had been in to consult with her. She told me I was the first. I have my derby edge.

59th Derby Off to a Quick and Predictably Nutty Start

It's the derby and that is all you need to know.
(September 2004)

G OOD WEATHER AND good fishing combined for a quick start to the 59th annual Martha's Vineyard Striped Bass and Bluefish Derby. A number of the approximately three thousand fishermen expected to enter the tournament left the starting gate at 12:01 am, Sunday, the official opening of the derby in an early effort to catch the largest bonito, false albacore, bluefish, and striped bass from boat and shore.

People familiar with the month-long contest know that derby fishermen are a strange lot. They describe events and tell stories that most non-fishermen react to as quite crazy stuff. But because most derby fishermen speak to other fishermen, it is generally accepted as quite normal.

I ran into Bob "Hawkeye" Jacobs of Oak Bluffs at the weigh station He told me about his efforts to retrieve a false albacore he hooked while fishing from Memorial Wharf in Edgartown. I relate his derby story.

Armed with butterfish, mackerel, and eels for bait, Bob, a computer programmer, was itching to begin his derby just after midnight fishing from the beach. By the time the sun rose Sunday

Bob "Hawkeye" Jacobs on
Memorial Wharf in Edgartown.

morning he had one bluefish to weigh in and went looking for a
false albacore, a trip that brought him to one of his regular fishing
spots on Memorial Wharf in Edgartown.

When Bob arrived he heard from some of his fellow wharf
rats that several big albies, including a 10- and a 12-pounder, had
already been caught. He was late but hopeful as he set about catching fresh butterfish, a prime bait for albies and bonito.

It took a little longer than he expected, but he got his bait. As
he went to cast out a live butterfish, he saw the Pied Piper, a small
passenger ferry which operates between Edgartown Harbor and
Falmouth Harbor, approaching the wharf on its regular run. The
ferry pulled up on the south end of the wharf, leaving Bob with
some dock space on the Chappy ferry end. He tossed his bait out.
Within minutes he hooked a big albie.

A false albacore is essentially a mini-tuna with proportionate
strength and speed. Even a small albie in the eight-pound range

can run off hundreds of yards of line before a fisherman has time to react. In addition to the normal challenges of landing a big albie, Edgartown Harbor adds numerous obstacles, including powerboats, sailboats, and fixed moorings. And then there is the Chappy ferry which runs back and forth across the harbor. Luckily for derby wharf rats hooked up to a big fish, the ferry captains are, for the most part, a sympathetic lot.

"I thought I was in pretty good shape," Bob said, "because he headed towards the Chappy ferry and the driver stopped the ferry for me."

Bob said that with one exception, the ferry captains do their best not to cut off fishermen. "Bobby Gilkes and Brad [Fligor], all the other drivers, if they see you have a fish on they stop the ferry for you, I mean they are wonderful that way."

The albie stopped, turned, and ran up into the harbor towards the Edgartown Yacht Club and the shore "in overdrive." Bob could only hang on and keep his rod tip up as his line went tight around the bow of the docked Pied Piper.

"Now I knew I had a problem," Bob said. Quickly he opened the bail on his fishing reel to relieve line tension and hopped up on the boat figuring his only chance would be to get his line off the bow and work his way to the stern of the vessel.

Bob began reeling in line. The plan was working until he realized his line led under the midsection of the boat and the fish was hung up. He could still feel the big albie pulsing at the end of his line.

All of this activity went unseen by the regular wharf rats who are part of an unofficial club each derby. Bob asked an accommodating crew member to tell one of the fishermen to bring the long handled net the regulars keep handy. Dennis Gough of West Tisbury, came on board with the net.

Despite several efforts to use his rod tip to free the fish, the line remained pinned under the boat. Unwilling to break off his fish Bob reviewed his options.

"I realized that I had my mask, my fins and my snorkel in my car," Bob said. "I thought, maybe if put on my skin-diving equipment I can get down there and free it, then get back on the wharf, jump back on the boat and play him."

And that seemed reasonable, I asked? "Yeah, it did," Bob said.

Bob asked Dennis to grab his mask and snorkel from his car. He explained to me that it was a beautiful hot day and slack tide.

Bob and Dennis talked over the best strategy in order to avoid violating derby rules which prohibit someone else touching the line during the fight. They decided Bob should lean his rod against the boat and loosen the reel's drag.

I asked Bob if Dennis reacted to him as though he were the slightest bit crazy?

"No, he didn't," Bob said. "Not at all."

Dennis went to get the mask and snorkel out of Bob's car. Bob stripped down to his pants and emptied his pockets. Pointing to a larger unseen derby force at work, Bob said, "Somehow, there was a Ziploc food storage bag laying on the boat passenger bench where I was. It was like it was put there just to store the stuff in my pocket."

Now you might wonder what the crew was thinking about all this fishing activity. Bob said that when he first boarded the boat and began trying to free his fish one crew member did get a bit exercised.

"She comes running up at me, really nasty, really challenging and she goes, 'Sir, what are you doing on our boat?'

"And I just said to her, 'yeah, I have a fish on.' And then I tuned her out. And I realized later, yeah, a fish on, that explains it."

Other crew members proved more accommodating as Bob donned his mask and snorkel. He jumped in the water. It is hard to know what the fish thought at that point.

But there was a problem. The line went under the center of the boat, requiring a deeper dive than Bob had expected and he had not asked Dennis to bring his swim fins, which were still in the car.

Bob made a few quick dives to assess the situation. The water was murky. He was hesitant to dive under the midsection of the boat without fins.

Bob thought about asking Dennis to get the fins but as he treaded water a crew member told him, "You've got one minute."

He went under and came up. "You've got 30 seconds," said the crew member, "we've got to stay on our schedule."

The Pied Piper pulled away from the dock with Bob's derby hope.

Later, talking like he could have been a contender if only he had had his fins, Bob said, "I think I ran out of time."

Bob, who fished his first derby in 1974, admitted that it might be difficult for those unfamiliar with how difficult and time consuming it is to catch a big albie to understand his swim.

"It might not be that easy to make them really understand," said Bob. "I can explain why it was worth the effort to me, maybe, but I do not know that anybody else would agree."

"I know how hard it is to find a big albie, it might take me two weeks to find a big albie, and there I had one on the end of my line."

No matter how inexplicable the derby may be to the uninitiated, sometimes derby fishermen and other people intersect in odd ways. Bob was back at Memorial Wharf bait fishing with another fisherman on Monday evening when a young woman in her twenties walked up highly agitated and near tears.

Speaking with an accent she asked, "Do either one of you have a big hook?"

"Big hook?" Bob said. "Why do you need a big hook?

"My bicycle fell in the water. Can you catch my bicycle?"

Always ready to help a European damsel in distress, Bob and his pal Dom rigged a big treble hook used for snagging bunker to a piece of clothes line, part of the flotsam and jetsam in Bob's vehicle.

Dom began fishing for the bicycle. Within a few minutes he hooked something.

"He starts pulling it up," Bob said, "and it is one of those long tools used to open up manhole covers, and it's attached to a wheel. Son of a gun, it is a bicycle, but it's not hers. It's a different bicycle."

The guys go back to fishing unsuccessfully for the woman's bike. And Bob gets an idea. He has a mask, fins and snorkel in his car. But he was not anxious to go back in the water a second day in a row.

Luckily, Dom snagged a mountain bicycle, the correct one, and brought it to the surface.

"She was just so grateful," Bob said. "I think it was a rental."

The Derby Fates Favor
Island Eighth Grader

Chris Morris combined skill and luck to walk away a winner.
(October 2007)

IT IS LIKELY that many of the more than 3,000 fishermen who fished day and night in the 62nd Martha's Vineyard Striped Bass and Bluefish Derby that ended Saturday looked up at a star-filled sky with the hope that he or she would catch a winning fish.

A few fishermen, the better students of ancient Greek history among us, might have been able to pick out a constellation. The gods and goddesses of Greek mythology included three sisters, the Moirae, the goddesses of destiny who assigned each person his or her fate.

The derby has a mythology. It is built on 62 years of big fish caught and big fish lost; legendary fishermen and magical places with names like Squibnocket and Wasque and Devil's Bridge.

And the derby has its fates. How else to explain the Island boat fisherman who caught a grand leader fish and won the truck grand prize for the second year in a row; or the Oak Bluffs eighth grader who caught and lost and caught again the heaviest bluefish? Or the man who caught the winning bluefish that wasn't?

And the derby has its grandmothers. There is no substitute for a grandmother's intuition.

As did many fishermen, Tom Robinson and I fished to the end of the derby Saturday night. I really wanted to go home, but I could not. The derby does that to you.

Tom and I were sitting on the beach at West Chop. I calculated that we had to fish until 9:30 pm. After that I said we would be unable to make the weigh station in Edgartown before the weigh master rang the bell at 10 pm to officially end the derby.

In a delirious afterthought that reflected the sort of irrational beliefs that fuel derby fishermen, I told Tom that if one of us did catch a winning fish we could just throw our rods up on the beach and run for the truck. Tom assured me he could make it to Edgartown in 15 minutes. I reasoned that no Island police officer would ever stand in the way of a derby fisherman rushing to the last weigh-in.

Tom said that wouldn't matter because we would lose precious minutes explaining the story to the policeman. I said we would just have to go for it and explain the story to the officers chasing us once we arrived. Thankfully my OJ in a white Bronco with a derby fish scenario did not play out. We said "no mas" and went home.

The official five-week weigh-in tally was 1,413 bluefish, 432 bonito, 509 albies, and 745 striped bass. My sense is that the shore fishing for bluefish, striped bass, and bonito was slow.

The big fish story was the big weight story. Lev Wlodyka, who would end up setting a new grand slam record, caught a 57.56 pound bass that contained ten lead weights. After much deliberation, derby officials concluded the fish likely ingested the weights as a result of a fishing technique known as yo-yoing, in which a lead weight is inserted into the stomach of a bait fish, such as menhaden, and the bait is then bounced off the bottom. On occasion, the fish takes the bait but is not hooked.

The way in which the derby committee dealt with the issue said something about the tribal nature of a fishing contest that reflects the divisions, alliances, and values of the Island community. And the value of not getting lawyers involved.

In Afghanistan, tribal leaders convene what is called a "loya jirga" (literally, a "grand assembly") to deal with important issues. On the Vineyard the derby convenes a committee meeting with representatives of the Menemsha clans, charter warlords, and tribal members from Oak Bluffs and Edgartown sheiks to hash out issues. Somehow it all works out and it did in the 62nd derby.

On Sunday afternoon, approximately 300 Derby fishermen, well-wishers, and family members gathered for the derby awards ceremony in the Outerland nightclub. Those gathered included the eight grand leaders, the four boat and four shore fishermen who had caught the heaviest fish of each of the derby's four species. The ceremony began with introductions by long-time derby president Ed Jerome and tireless committee chairman John Custer. One by one fishermen of all ages, many already familiar to the crowd, took to the stage to receive awards in numerous categories.

But that was all a prelude to the big moment when Ed would call the eight grand leaders up to the stage.

Each grand leader reaches into a box and picks a number that determines his or her place in the four-person line up in the boat and shore divisions. In turn each person picks a key. One by one Ed takes the key and inserts it into a padlock held next to a microphone and tries to turn the key.

On Sunday the boat division holder of the key that opened the lock would win a 2008 Chevy Silverado 4X4, courtesy of the Clay Family Dealerships and that wonderful Chappy fishing couple, Bob and Fran Clay. The shore fisherman with the right key stood to win a 19-foot Boston Whaler Montauk, Mercury outboard, and trailer, courtesy of the Derby and Boston Whaler.

Among the eight grand leaders on stage that day hoping to win a new truck or boat were two brothers who fish hard together,

Zeb Tilton, who caught a winning 56.51-pound boat striped bass, and Zachary Tilton, whose 40.61-pounder topped the shore bass division.

For Clark Goff Jr., a Chilmarker who now lives in Virginia, it must have seemed like a dream. The first albie he ever caught weighed 15.86 pounds, and there he was up on stage as his parents, Pam and Clark Goff, looked on from the seats in front.

Geoff Codding, boat bonito winner, had been on stage only the year before with a winning boat albie. He arrived for Sunday's ceremony in the truck he won that day. Up until last year the Derby fates had not been kind to Geoff, who had been bumped out of the grand leader spot to second place eight times.

The fates were certainly looking out for 13-year-old Christopher Morris who earned his place among the adults on stage when he caught an 11.70-pound shore bluefish that put him in the grand leader spot.

Chris fishes with his dad, Steve Morris, former derby chairman and owner of Dick's tackle shop in Oak Bluffs. The derby schedule was homework then fishing. Father and son were casting eels when Chris hooked a nice bluefish that broke his line. "So he re-tied and he started casting again," Steve said, "and darn if he didn't catch another one."

When Steve went to unhook the fish, he could not believe his eyes. "Chris," he shouted to his son, "it's got your other hook and eel in its mouth."

Unknown to Chris, a larger bluefish would be caught only two days before the end of the Derby but the fisherman had not registered in the derby.

A combination of fate, luck and fishing skill had assembled eight derby fishermen on stage Sunday. Bruce McIntosh was the first boat fisherman to hand Ed his key and wait apprehensively for the sound of a click as the lock snapped open. Zeb Tilton

was next. The crowd murmured with excitement when Sandy
Fisher, the third man in line handed Ed his key. It did not turn
and Sandy gave the last man in line a big hug as the crowd
roared.

Ed turned Geoff's key in the lock and it sprang open.

All attention focused on the shore fishermen. Chris handed
Ed his key as the crowd held their collective breath and the room
grew silent. Click!

Chris looked stunned as Ed, former Edgartown School principal, embraced the young boy. Steve stepped up on stage and gave
his favorite fishing partner a hug.

Asked for a comment, the most Chris could muster was, "This
is awesome."

Among those in the crowd shouting for joy was Emily Frank
of Edgartown, Christopher's grandmother. She almost did not

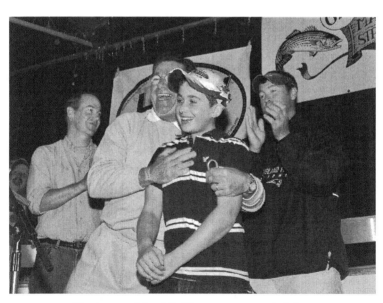

Derby president Ed Jerome congratulates
boat winner Chris Morris.

make the ceremony. Emily had made plans with her sister Mardell Francis to go off-Island Sunday to attend a nephew's baby shower. When Dottie Grant, Emily's friend heard about her plans to go off-Island she told her, "You're going to be sorry if he wins that boat."

"So I went to Mardell's," Emily said, "and I kept thinking about it and I thought, I can't go, he'll probably win that boat and then I'll be so mad that I wasn't there. So I took her to the boat, I went home and called Dottie, and she came and picked me up and we went up there to the ceremony."

Emily said she was watching Ed Jerome when he took her grandson's key and could tell it was going to open by the way his thumb was moving. "And I just let out a scream cause it went click. I was overwhelmed."

Derby luck runs in the family. Four years later in the 2011 derby, Steve Morris was the shore bluefish division leader and won the grand prize of a new boat. It was Steve's second trip to the podium. In 1983 he won the striped bass division to claim the grand prize.

Neptune Shines His Favors on Those Who Respect His Realm

Conrad Neumann thought his treasured hat was lost forever.
(August 2015)

A WELL-WORN FISHING HAT is as important a piece of fishing equipment as a rod and reel. Few derby fishermen would think of leaving home without their hats. Sufficiently aged and speckled with fish gore, squid ink, and pizza sauce, or adorned with the small fish pins the derby awards for making the daily board, a good hat is a prized talisman.

One of the Island's more distinctive style of fishing hats, one which has nothing to do with the derby, but is anchored in Island culture, is the swordfish cap. Years ago, when swordfish were plentiful and within a few days striking distance of Island boats, Menemsha supported a swordfishing fleet that relied on the harpoon, a strong arm, and good aim to catch fish found lolling on the surface of the ocean on a hot summer day. Spotting a basking swordfish was not easy.

The swordfish cap features a distinctive long, pointed brim that once served a practical purpose — other than making tourists look like geeks — it shaded the eyes, making it easier to spot fish in the glare of the sun. Just as not everyone should not wear a tank helmet (remember presidential candidate Mike Dukakis as Rocky the flying squirrel?), not everyone can carry off a swordfish cap. It requires a certain physical bearing and presence.

Conrad Neumann of Menemsha carries it off. His faded Poole's Fish Market hat sits on his head like it belongs there. Unfortunately, one day while fishing in a boat off Aquinnah between Squibnocket Point and Philbin Beach, it sat on his head a little too lightly, and a gust of wind blew it off his head into the water.

His sister, Jane Slater, related the story in her weekly town news column for the Vineyard Gazette. "The old, red, billed swordfish cap was a treasured bit of his wardrobe, and was sporting a derby button and a gold insignia pin given him in recognition of his descents in submersibles Alvin and NR-1, a nuclear research submersible," Jane said. "Needless to say, this was a loss to regret."

A little background is in order. Conrad is retired professor emeritus at the University of North Carolina, Chapel Hill, and conducted research "on the deposition of modern carbonate sediments in the lagoons, margins, and deep flanks of limestone platforms in the Florida-Bahama region, and used his findings to reconstruct the histories of ancient limestones and draw inferences about sea level fluctuations and climate change over geologic time," according to the university website.

Among his many dives, in 1971 he descended to depths of up to 700 meters in the Alvin, to the base of Little Bahama Bank and northeastern Straits of Florida. In other words, he traveled almost half a mile in a can to the cold, dark bottom of the ocean. That certainly rated a pin.

The hat was at the bottom of the ocean. But Neptune favors those who visit his realm.

About 10 days later, even as Conrad's hat was drifting in the ocean currents, Nick Wilbur, a new breed of young Island commercial fishermen, was teasing his friend Alec Gale, partner in Menemsha Fish House, a wholesale operation on Menemsha Harbor, about his catch during a recent tuna trip. Alec had hoped to also catch a swordfish, but only caught tuna. The obvious reason he was unsuccessful, Nick told Alec, was that he did not have a long-brimmed cap.

Later that day, Nick went spearfishing for tautog off the beach near the painted house, a local landmark so named for its multi-colored roof, just east of Philbin Beach in Aquinnah. In addition to tautog, he found a swordfish cap on the bottom of the sea floor.

Nick brought the hat and the fish to Michael Holtham, manager of Menemsha Fish House. The fish were sold; the hat was put on a counter.

Let me back up just a bit. Longtime Derby fishermen have their favored registration button numbers. Mike's favorite number is 2323.

The day before Nick came in with his long-brimmed catch, Mike had gone into Menemsha Texaco to register for the Derby. "When I went to sign up for it, they said, 'Sorry, that number's been taken by Conrad Neumann.'"

Mike was not perturbed, and had his daughter pick a new lucky number. The next day, when Nick came in with the hat, he saw a Derby registration button from a previous year pinned to the hat. The button number was 2324.

Mike had seen Conrad in his long-brimmed hat around the dock. The Derby number sequence was on the hat just one digit off the number Conrad had claimed.

"It was just too coincidental," Mike said. He put two and two together.

Mike returned the hat to Conrad, who was thrilled to get it back. Neptune smiled.

Deer Hunting

Island deer hunters gather at the state forest deer check
station on the opening day of the 2003 shotgun season.

Walter Ashley once spent a day and a half looking for a deer, because he knew he had hit it and knew it was dead. Asked why he spent so much time looking for that one deer, Walter said, "Because that is what you are supposed to do. You shot the animal, so you are responsible."

Contemplating Black Mambas and the Finer Points of Deer Urine

From his tree stand, a deer hunter reports from Chilmark. (December 2000)

I STARTED TO THINK of black mamba snakes. The mind tends to wander after a couple of hours of tedium while sitting in a tree stand during shotgun week waiting for a deer to come within range.

I had not seen a deer in two days of occupying my perch for several hours, morning and afternoon, approximately twelve feet up a tree near a break in a stone wall in Chilmark. My friend and hunting companion, Alley Moore, was sitting in a tree stand nearby and he was having no better luck.

Shots echoed near and far, letting me know that other hunters were having more success. The shots were revealing — more often than not a succession of shots indicates a hunter or hunters on the ground shooting at a running deer trying to make its escape. A single report is usually a well-aimed shot fired by a hunter from a tree stand. It carries a sense of finality.

Having killed a deer from the very same tree on the first morning of the season last year, my first ever deer, I thought I was in a good spot. Alley had also shot his first deer the previous year. Now I was beginning to think that maybe we had just been lucky.

Fishing and deer hunting have much in common. Sure, on occasion a novice walks down to the beach and catches a big striped bass, but it is the fishermen who take the time to learn their spots that catch most of the big fish. Hunting is no different.

The white tail deer relies on an extraordinary sense of smell, pinpoint hearing and keen eyesight for its survival. Deer bed down during the daytime hours in thick brush and travel to feeding areas as the sun begins to set. The most successful hunters understand how and why deer move and scout locations extensively to place themselves in a position to get a good shot. I had done none of that.

I began the six-day shotgun week enthusiastically and maybe just a bit overconfident based on my previous success and the fact that deer biologists said the Island deer herd is large and growing. Island bowhunters, the first to take part in the annual deer harvest, agreed with that assessment.

Gary BenDavid, an Oak Bluffs contractor and experienced bowhunter, had lent me a tree stand to use for the week. As I prepared to leave his garage Gary fiddled in a box of hunting gear. He found a small, brown plastic spray bottle and handed me a half-full, four-ounce "pro-size" bottle of "Hunter's Scent scrape juice."

Gary said to spray it around my stand to attract deer but he cautioned me to avoid getting any of the liquid on me. "It stinks like hell but it really works," Gary said.

I sat in my tree stand slowly turning my head as I scanned the surrounding thick brush for any sign of movement. Even when seated in a tree stand, a hunter must avoid making any sudden movement that would be detected by a deer. I shifted slightly in my uncomfortable seat and waited.

The previous evening on television I had watched a crazy Australian snake expert as he went in search of a black mamba. Why the hell anyone, even a crazy Aussie, would want to find one of these snakes, was beyond me, but before the show had fulfilled its intended purpose and I fell off to sleep I learned something about the black mamba.

These snakes grow to a length of fifteen feet, travel up to speeds of thirteen miles per hour and unlike many venomous snakes that try to get away from people, will aggressively attack and have been known to give chase. Sitting in my tree stand, even with no deer in sight, I was consoled by the thought that at least there were no black mambas in Chilmark. In fact, holding a Remington 870 shotgun loaded with five deer slugs I felt pretty damn safe.

As Alley and I neared the end of shotgun week we began to despair of taking a deer. One morning, after sitting in my tree since before sunrise for hours, I stood up to stretch my limbs. Unfortunately, I did not see two deer that were either bedded down close to me or were traveling through thick brush not more than thirty yards from me.

On Saturday, the last day of the season, Alley and I met before we went into our respective tree stands. I handed Alley the bottle of scrape juice and told him to spray it around his stand. We exited the woods after the sun had set without having had any success and met where we had parked.

"What is that stuff," Alley asked, referring to the scrape juice. "I smell like the restroom at Grand Central station."

The entire contents of the spray bottle had leaked out in the pocket of his blaze orange hunting vest. I assured him I had not played a joke and that the bottle cap had either loosened or the container had cracked. I tried not to laugh and indict myself but the odor was strong and unmistakable.

That evening Alley called me on his cell phone as he drove around trying to air out his car. He said that when he had arrived home he didn't dare bring his vest in the house so he left it outside on his back porch. Then he let his dog, Emmett, a black Lab out.

When he went to fetch the vest to wash it he discovered that Emmett, upon smelling the vest, had taken upon himself to "mark it," and peed on it. "It was a real hosing," Alley told me. The temperature had dropped and the entire vest was a frozen dog and deer pee sculpture.

This is interesting, I thought — after I stopped laughing.

So the next day I made a call to Scrape Juice Hunting products in Perry, Ga., manufactures of Bow Hunters Scent and a range of products used by successful bowhunters around the country. Dennis Lewis, the owner of the company for the past four years an accomplished bowhunter, answered the phone. He told me he does a lot of business in Massachusetts.

I explained that I had spent a week sitting in a tree stand with just a cold to show for it. In a thick Georgia accent he put it all in perspective for me: "At least ya gettin' ta hunt."

When he is not selling his hunting scent products Dennis runs a drugstore in Perry, a town with a population of about 20,000. He also writes a hunting column for the local newspaper.

Dennis said he learned about the "scrape juice bowhunter setup" from a man in his hunting club who had killed several nice trophy bucks. The hunter gave a bottle to Dennis that he used to make a scent trail down to his stand. It soon proved its effectiveness. Ignoring Dennis's human scent a buck walked down the same trail. Dennis missed the shot but that did not deter the buck.

"Now I watched him stop in the trail that I had walked down — now this buck's spooked — he knows somethin' bad happened because the arrow broke, he broke it when he run off because it went in between his legs — well, he was blowin', stompin', carryin' on and gettin' out of there, but when he hit that scent trail I watched him put his nose to the ground and walk right back to the base of my tree and I said, 'wow,' this stuff is awesome to bring a spooked buck back."

"So I killed that deer along with two others."

Dennis was written up in a magazine article in which he mentioned the product. The owner of the scent company called him up to thank him and later, when the owner got ready to retire, he offered Dennis the chance to buy the company.

"We bottle the real stuff," Dennis told me. That would be urine from 129 leased whitetail deer on a deer farm. In the tone of a fine vintner confident his wine is derived from the best grapes, Dennis explained that the owner of the farm is a personal friend.

"I actually buy 100 percent white tail deer urine from him and we don't cut it and we don't add preservatives," he said.

However, he added, he does several things to enhance the product. Unwilling to share the details of his trade secrets he did volunteer that the formula is spiced by using various deer gland extractions and includes a secret additive developed by a Georgia trapper that was handed down to the originators of the scrape juice company when it began production in 1984.

Dennis said there are a lot of scents on the market but his company does not add any preservatives. Organic, I guess.

He said he may never be able to sell to a large chain store such as Wal-Mart, "because you've got to have enough of the real stuff to actually bottle the real thing."

Freshness counts as well. According to a description on the company website, scrapejuice.com, "all whitetail deer lures are shipped to you within three days of collection. You can't get much fresher than that unless you want to collect it yourself!"

I asked Dennis if he wasn't the least bit curious why some guy from Martha's Vineyard had called him to talk about deer scent. Polite in that charming southern manner, he admitted he had wondered about it.

So I told him the story about the container that leaked and the dog-deer-pee sculpture. "Oh my God," he said with a laugh. Almost apologetic, he explained, "It will attract any animal — that it will do."

He quickly added, "I hate you didn't get a deer." I said that had more to do with my inexperience than his product.

He said that deer have an acute sense of smell, which is one of the reasons they are so difficult to hunt and the reason his product has found a ready market. He offered to send me a scent sampler.

Just to satisfy my intellectual curiosity, I called Filene's department store and was connected to the fragrance department. A woman speaking with a European accent (which I assumed was a required skill) answered the telephone.

"What can I purchase for $15 a bottle?" I asked.

"Oh," she said with just a hint of shock, "We have nothing like that."

I asked her what I would have to spend to smell good. She told me that some French perfumes easily cost more than $100 but that a 1.7 ounce bottle of Calvin Klein eau de toilette (which is French for diluted perfume) would cost $42.

At that price I concluded that a four ounce undiluted bottle of "eau de scrape juice" is a pretty good bargain. I guess it just depends on the quarry.

Deer Hunter Remains Undaunted by the Challenge of a Flintlock

Hunt with a muzzleloader and you will gain a new respect for those who relied on this weapon for food and protection. (October 2002)

I SPENT A LOT of time last week sitting in a tree in Chilmark think-ing about Captain Meriwether Lewis and Captain William Clark, leaders of the famed expedition that provided early American colo-nists with their first glimpse of what lay beyond the Mississippi River.

Not that I purposely climb up a tree to think. But I find that if I spend any amount of time in one place, that is what I do, and sitting in a deer stand attached to a tree approximately 12 feet up is where I was.

My attention to Lewis and Clark during my mental wander-ings was related to the fact that I was holding a Pennsylvania flint-lock muzzle-loading rifle, similar in most respects to the type of weapon carried by both men and their party, known as the Corps of Discovery, during their hazard-filled journey to the Pacific northwest and back between 1803 and 1806. More than 200 hun-dred years later I was determined to shoot a deer with a flintlock during the state muzzleloader season.

Luckily for me, I was not facing down a band of Yankton Sioux Indians on the Missouri River, hunting for elk and deer in order to survive a trek through the Rockies, or trying to stop a charging grizzly beer on the Great Plains. I was simply sitting in a tree in Chilmark hoping to shoot a white tailed deer, and I did not realize that I had forgotten to load my rifle since I had fired it days before for the benefit of a friend's son.

Had a deer walked by, I would have pulled the trigger and heard a quick pffft when the powder in the firing pan ignited . . . and nothing else. The only consequences of my forgetfulness would have been a good laugh at my expense by my hunting partner, Cooper Gilkes of Edgartown, who was armed with a far more modern blackpowder rifle equipped with a telescopic sight.

At one time, the so-called primitive weapons season was simply a three-day afterthought provided by state wildlife officials after the traditional shotgun season, for people who enjoyed hunting with one-shot muskets that relied on pre-Civil War ignition systems. Basically, flint striking metal was the method used to ignite a powder charge in firearms from the early 1600s until the introduction of the percussion cap in the mid-1800s.

As the numbers of deer and of black-powder enthusiasts increased, the state lengthened the season to one week, and then in a major change this year extended it to Dec. 31 providing a full two and a half weeks of hunting. In addition, restrictions were dropped that prohibited more reliable and technologically advanced ignitions systems, telescopic scopes, and modern style bullets, giving hunters a much better chance of taking a deer with one shot.

As do many hunters I enjoy the hunting experience as much as the end result of fresh game for the dinner table. This is why I wanted to see if I could take a deer using only my flintlock, before the season ended on the last day of the year.

Last season, I brought the rifle up on one of four does standing within 20 yards of my stand, but when I pulled the trigger, the flint failed to create a spark to ignite the powder. That was a result of my tinkering the night before, during which I had left too wide a space between the flint and the frizzen, the hard metal plate which when struck by the flint creates the sparks that ignite a small charge of powder in the pan, touching off the main charge.

According to the book "Undaunted Courage," author Stephen E. Ambrose's account of the Lewis and Clark expedition (Simon and Schuster), Captain Lewis stopped at Harpers Ferry, Va., site of the U.S. Army's arsenal, on March 15, 1803, to pick up what were then the top-of-the-line armaments for his party, fifteen muzzle-loading, flintlock, long-barreled rifles, sometimes called "Kentucky rifles" but more properly "Pennsylvania rifles."

"They were absolutely dependable — the U.S. Model 1803, the first rifle specifically designed for the U.S. Army, .54-caliber, with a thirty-three-inch barrel. Lewis referred to these weapons as short rifles, for they were considerably shorter than the civilian Pennsylvania rifle. The Model 1803 delivered a lead slug on target with sufficient velocity to kill a deer at a range of about a hundred yards. An expert could get off two aimed shots in one minute."

I was hunting with a Pennsylvania Hunter manufactured by the Thompson/Center Arms Company of New Hampshire, one of the major manufacturers of traditional and modern black-powder firearms. The rifle weighs 7.5 pounds, is 45 inches in length with a 28-inch barrel, and fires a .50-caliber round lead ball. As for two well aimed shots, I need five stress-free minutes.

Although two centuries removed, the mechanics of loading and firing my rifle remain the same. After a charge of powder is poured into the muzzle of the barrel, a lead ball is placed on a lubricated cloth patch that helps seal in gases, and the ball is pushed down the barrel with a ramrod until it is firmly seated on the powder. A small charge of powder is put into the flashpan. The flint is held by a clamp and cocked back. When the trigger is pulled the flint strikes the lifting frizzen and sends a shower of sparks into the powder in the pan. If all goes well, the powder in the pan ignites the powder in the barrel and the rifle fires almost instantaneously.

According to Mr. Ambrose, Captain Lewis was an excellent shot, particularly when using his walking stick as a rifle rest. "If the target was within a hundred yards and bigger than a mouse, he usually got it."

Practicing with my rifle at the rod and gun club range, I initially was unable to hit a target the size of an aardvark at 25 yards. The problem was an unconscious flinch that I could stop only by concentrating on holding the target in my sights through the flash of the primer charge igniting. A not uncommon problem for people new to a flintlock.

The men of the Lewis and Clark expedition did little flinching, even in the face of their first encounter with a grizzly bear. Initially, Captain Lewis had been anxious to meet up with an animal he had heard so much about from traders and Indians, although "It gave him a bit of pause that the Indians, before attacking a grizzly, went through all the rituals they commonly used before going on a war party."

After the expedition's first two encounters with grizzlies, including one bear estimated at over 500 pounds that took five rifle balls before dropping, Lewis wrote in his journal: "I find that the curiossity of our party is pretty well satisfyed with rispect to this anamal."

In one of the most memorable and dangerous battles of the trip, six men attacked a bear they had spotted on a river bank. "Four men fired simultaneously, while two soldiers held their rifles in reserve. All four balls hit the mark, two passing through the lungs."

The bear charged with open mouth. The two-man reserve force fired, each man hitting the bear, but that only slowed it down for an instant, and it took after several of the men.

The others reloaded and fired. Although hit several more times, the bear went after two men, "who threw away their rifles and pouches and dived into the river, from a perpendicular bank of near twenty feet.

"The bear jumped in after them. He was about to reach one of the swimmers when a soldier on the bank finally shot him through the head and killed him."

Throughout their journey, the men of an expedition that helped shape the destiny of our country relied on their hunting and outdoor skills to survive. The opportunity to hunt with a traditional flintlock provides me with one small measure of just how considerable those skills were.

Sitting in my tree I wondered if I could aim well enough to hit a grizzly bear closing on my friend Coop. I figured he would prefer to take his chances swimming. And with only two days to go I sat waiting for a deer.

Island Archers Follow in the Footsteps of Past Hunters

The weaponry has evolved but the required instincts and skills remain the same.
(November 2005)

THOUSANDS OF YEARS ago a prehistoric hunter figured out that hurling a straight tree branch tipped with a sharp piece of stone at an animal that tasted good was one way to put food on the fire pit. Before long an overachieving Cro-Magnon built a bow and arrow. Word got around even without instant messaging.

According to one report, examples of ancient bows and arrows have been discovered in every part of the world except Australia, probably because the boomerang is so cool.

Ancient bows were usually made of wood branches or saplings with strings made of animal hide and likely cost a few clamshells. The cost of a modern compound bow outfitted with a fiber-optic sight, custom bow string and carbon arrows tipped with razor sharp steel points easily reaches $1,000. That's a lot of clams.

Still, despite advances in bow hunting weaponry the basic hunting skills experienced Island hunters rely on during the state's six-week deer archery season that began Oct. 17 are not that much different from those Adam used after he told Eve he was not going to be a vegan. Hitting a deer with an arrow requires proper shooting technique and concentration. That can only come with practice.

Tracking and finding an animal that has been shot requires skills that can only come from experience. Some hunters are better at it than others.

Last archery season, I was deep in a Chilmark swamp entangled in briars and thickets despairing of finding any sign of a large buck I had arrowed earlier that morning. The cell phone in my pocket rang. "Where are you," Ned Casey said. "I found blood up by the stone wall."

The sense of gloom that had settled over the excitement I had felt hours earlier began to lift. Needing help, I had called Ned and explained what had happened. He said he would be right up to help and assured me we would find my deer.

Ned, an experienced hunter, had found a small droplet of blood on a stone in a gap in a stonewall hundreds of yards from where I shot the deer. Small drops became larger drops that led us to the buck.

Put aside the phone and the scent-free Cabela's clothing we wore, and Ned and I were following in the footsteps of hunters throughout the ages. The quarry may have been deer instead of mastodon, but the object was the same — to find and read the signs that indicate how well an animal has been hit and the direction it went.

Walter Ashley of Oak Bluffs, a state certified hunter safety instructor, has been bowhunting for more than 30 years. Lean and spare in his comments and look, Walter is an expert marksman and hunter.

During archery season Walter voluntarily checks in deer taken by hunters for the state Division of Fisheries and Wildlife. He records data and sells doe permits at his small engine repair shop, C & W Power Equipment off Airport Road in Edgartown. The shop is a focal point of bow hunting activity and stories.

I spoke with Walter and Ned about some of the skills it takes to recover a deer. Both agreed that finding a deer begins with shot placement, a critical element when hunting with a bow.

The bow hunter must think in terms of the arrow's angle of entry and exit in order to ensure the razor sharp broadhead hits a vital spot. That takes patience, concentration and a willingness to pass up a poor shot opportunity.

Once the arrow is released it is imperative that the hunter focus on the arrow's flight. Seeing where a deer was struck can help a hunter determine how far the animal may go before it lays down and expires. A well-struck deer sometimes falls dead within sight of an archer. But even a mortally wounded deer is capable of running out of sight.

A good tracker reads his or her arrow. An arrow covered with blood and small bubbles indicates a lung hit and a mortally wounded deer. Dark blood indicates a liver shot. An arrow covered with food matter indicates the deer was likely hit behind the lungs in the intestinal area. Even the color of the hair on the arrow can be read for signs.

Often a deer that has been shot will go a short distance and bed down in heavy cover. If it is well hit it will go no farther as long as it is not disturbed.

"Always wait," Walter said. How long depends on the type of hit. At a minimum, a hunter should wait 30 minutes to avoid spooking a deer.

"The problem with going after it when you shouldn't is you take the chance of losing it," said Walter, "because it is just going to get up and keep moving and moving."

A poorly hit deer must often be left to rest overnight. But every situation is different. A forecast of rain or snow, which can destroy a trail, leaves the hunter with no option but to go after a deer.

Tracking a deer requires attention to detail. Broken twigs and branches provide direction; how high blood is found on a branch indicates where an animal was hit which may not always correspond to what a hunter thinks he saw.

"Slow and easy," Walter said, is the best way to approach tracking an animal. "Take your time before you start, and then when you do start, go easy."

What to do when the obvious signs run out? "Then you stop and you look," said Walter. " Any broken branches, any runs, any little holes in bull briar patches, again, slow and easy."

Ned Casey grew up hunting birds, rabbit and deer in western Massachusetts with his father and brothers. His hunting education began when he shot his first deer, a big doe, with a Red Wing Hunter bow when he was 15 years old while hunting near his house by the Quabbin Reservoir. He was alone but managed to clean the deer having watched what other people did. He dragged the deer out of the woods. His mother saw him out the window. "I was covered with blood and she thought something had happened to me," said Ned, "and she started to scream. I said no, no Ma, I got a deer."

Ned said the key to finding a deer is the discipline it takes to pick an aiming spot on the deer and watch where the arrow hits without pulling your head away, and then to mark the spot where the animal was standing when it was hit and where it goes by picking out recognizable landmarks.

"When you climb down from the tree it looks totally different from when you are up in a tree," Ned said.

Tracking a deer requires patience and a willingness to inspect the ground inch by inch. Ned said it does happen that despite a hunter's best efforts and many hours spent looking, there are no signs to follow and a deer cannot be located. While not recovering a deer is a part of hunting and something he and many other hunters have experienced, it is never easy to accept. It all begins with the basics, he said.

"You are going to be excited, but don't be excited to the point where you are going to make a poor choice of a shot," Ned said.

"Because, then you do not have the satisfaction of knowing that you placed a good shot and the real work begins."

Ned and Walter highlighted the obligation hunters have to make the best effort to recover an animal after it has been shot.

"A lot of guys just give up too soon," Ned said. "We have a responsibility as hunters to follow through as much as we can."

Walter once spent a day and a half looking for a deer, because he knew he had hit it and knew it was dead. Asked why he spent so much time looking for that one deer, Walter said, "Because that is what you are supposed to do. You shot the animal, so you are responsible."

A Deer Hunter Tallies Up the Years

Shotgun week rekindles old traditions as Islanders take to the woods in pursuit of deer.
(December 2015)

Midway through the two-week deer shotgun season that began on Monday, I will turn 65 years old. The fact that this will occur on a treestand I carried into the woods and hauled up an oak tree by myself gives me some small comfort — as well as the fact that should I fall from the treestand, I am now covered by Medicare.

For those of you who must pay out of pocket to repair limbs, I highly recommend not trusting your body parts, or your life, to an aging stand — most hunting accidents involve falls, not weapons.

I was reminded of the risks at the start of bow season when I stepped onto a stand I had just placed in a tree. The platform support cables looked fine, but the corrosion was inside the plastic sleeve and not visible to me. One of the cables snapped. Luckily, I was strapped to a safety line and the other cable held.

I had tried to squeeze one more season out of an old stand. Is it worth it when a new stand can be had for under $200? Do the math using this formula: X new stands = 1 trip to the ER.

Another consequence of hanging onto stands too long, or buying cheap stands, is noise. This season I was bedeviled by squeaking stands. As any deer hunter knows, deer have an uncanny ability to pick up any unnatural sounds. A deer will ignore a squirrel frat party and traffic sounds, but jump at one click or squeak.

For the past five years I used a Summit Viper aluminum climbing stand that allowed me to shimmy up any straight tree with branches small enough for me to trim off with a small handsaw. This season the platform slats began to squeak no matter which way I shifted my weight. When I contacted the company, I learned that the warranty expired after five years.

Some quick research brought me to Lone Wolf, a family-owned company based in Illinois that produces high-quality tree stands. Serious hunters I know swear by them. I had my eye on the Hand Climber II, an easily packable stand that would give me good mobility, something the Viper, with its large profile, did not. Looking online, I read several comments from people who mentioned the need to be physically fit to use the climber. With a temperamental back and a bad shoulder, I was suddenly faced with a new consideration when purchasing hunting gear — I'm getting old.

I once thought of aging as something that happened to other people. It was theoretical. Not anymore. I called Matt Gamache of Vineyard Haven. Matt, a very fit builder, owned a Lone Wolf climber and I wanted to try it out. I had no problem with a test drive up a tree in Matt's backyard, which led me to happily conclude that I am in the upper percentile of fit old people. That was reassuring.

Over the course of the six-week archery season that ended last week, I shot one deer. I ought to have been able to take a very nice buck. The deer stopped about 10 yards broadside from me, but my shoulder ached and I was physically unable to draw my bowstring back. Too much abuse over the years had taken a toll.

The archery season was not a total loss. One afternoon, just after the sun went down and as the day disappeared, I watched the outline of two bucks as they closed with each other and begin to spar. As it grew dark I could no longer make out their silhouettes, but I sat in my stand and listened to the violent clatter of their antlers not more than 40 yards from my tree, while whippoorwills sang out from a nearby swamp.

My wife Norma has accepted the fact that during hunting season, my focus will be on hunting and not much else. And she appreciates the fact that my passion keeps me outdoors and not underfoot and in her space — most of the time.

Early in the archery season and on a day off, rain and summer-like temperatures kicked me out of the woods shortly after 8 am. Feeling slightly guilty, I told Norma I would accomplish at least one project: "I'll move all my summer shirts out of the closet, and move up my warmer shirts," I said.

She cringed at the thought and tried to dissuade me, recognizing she would likely have to retrace my steps to bring some order to the household. The closet accomplished, I moved on to my drawers. I had embarked on a voyage of discovery.

"Where's this been?" I said to Norma, "And this?" as I held up one piece of clothing and another.

Norma patiently explained that the thermal undershirt I held up like a long-lost friend had in fact been there all along, as had all of the other T shirts bearing various logos and phrases.

"What do you do," she said, "just take whatever is on top?"

And that was the answer. Each week the top layer circulated, and the bottom layer of clothing never moved. I had discovered a new wardrobe of familiar clothes.

On Sunday, I rearranged my hunting clothing in preparation for shotgun week. Out came the blaze orange and the warm clothing. Monday morning, I woke up well before dawn, anxious to get out to the woods, one of many eager hunters. For members of the Island's hunting fraternity, shotgun week is an opportunity to pursue deer with family and friends, in many cases carrying on an annual tradition. In between the day's hunts, there will be plenty of time to swap stories over breakfast and lunch.

One day this week, I will head out into the thick woods with my new Lone Wolf hand climber. The stand is exceptionally well built, and I figure it will still be capable of going up a tree long after I am not, but I plan to keep going up that tree as long as I can.

The Primitive Pursuit of Success on Martha's Vineyard

On the last day of the hunting season, a hunter entered the woods aiming to fulfill his long-talked-about goal to bag a deer with a flintlock.
(January 2016)

H UNT OR FISH long enough, and you will begin to repeat the same stories, complaints, and dreams so that even your most patient friends, or spouse, will ask you to stop.

My wife, Norma, stopped listening to my hunting stories a long time ago: "Blah, blah, blah, then the deer did this and then the deer did that, and then I shot it — oh no, I missed it," is pretty much how she sums up the evening telephone conversations she overhears in our living room that take on a ritualistic quality over the course of a hunting season.

Prior to my hesitant adoption of texting technology, it was customary for my friends and me to actually talk to each other most every evening about that day's hunt — what we saw or did not see, and any success we might have had.

I still have phone conversations, but now I am just as likely to receive a brief text: "saw nothin … doe too far away … goin in the morn?"

The one benefit of texting is that a hunter can communicate with nearby hunters quietly — assuming he or she remembers to silence the chime that will send any deer fleeing. I have found that a text message is quite a handy way, when I am fortunate enough to have shot a deer, to summon help to drag it out of the woods.

My fondness for the English language and unenthusiastic embrace of smartphone technology moves me to pay attention to spelling and punctuation when I send text messages. I am clearly in the minority.

Eons ago, hunters in pursuit of game communicated via grunts. Well, we have come full circle. The equivalent of the prehistoric grunt is the modern text message.

AAR (at any rate), with days to go before the end of the 2015 deer hunting season that began on Oct. 19, I was determined to bag a deer with my flintlock rifle. I told Alley Moore about my plan — we were actually speaking to each other — and Alley reminded me, "You've been saying the same thing for years." *Et tu*, Alley.

A quick check of past columns finds that I first began talking about my flintlock goal 15 years ago, when the so-called primitive firearms season lasted six days rather than sixteen, and I first had the opportunity to hunt with a Pennsylvania long rifle manufactured by the Thompson/Center Arms Co., a small manufacturer in New Hampshire, since acquired by the famed Smith & Wesson Co. of Springfield.

I still have the rifle, which weighs 7.5 pounds, is 45 inches in length, and fires a 50-caliber bullet from a barrel with a 1:66-inch twist. It differs little from the type of weapon used by Captain Meriwether Lewis and Captain William Clark, leaders of the famed Corps of Discovery, during their hazardous journey to the Pacific Northwest and back between 1803 and 1806, which gave early American colonists their first glimpse of what lay beyond the Mississippi River.

Flintlock firearms were in use from the early 1600s until the introduction of the percussion cap in the mid-1800s. Knowing how to charge the weapon is a valuable skill. Too little powder in the priming pan and there may be no ignition when the flint strikes the hard steel plate known as a frizzen, creating a shower of sparks. Too much powder can cause a significant delay before the main charge ignites, which can affect aim.

Anyone who fires a flintlock gains a new respect for such phrases as "flash in the pan" and "hang fire." In season, most hunters, me included, use muzzleloaders that incorporate modern technology, will reliably fire each time, and with a good scope can take a deer out to 150 yards, sometimes farther.

According to "Undaunted Courage," Stephen E. Ambrose's account of the Lewis and Clark expedition (Simon and Schuster), Captain Lewis stopped at Harper's Ferry, Va., site of the U.S. Army's arsenal, on March 15, 1803, to pick up for his party what were then the top-of-the-line armaments, 15 muzzle-loading, flintlock, long-barreled rifles, sometimes called "Kentucky rifles" but more properly "Pennsylvania rifles."

"The Model 1803 delivered a lead slug on target with sufficient velocity to kill a deer at a range of about a hundred yards. An expert could get off two aimed shots in one minute."

Early Thursday morning on the last day of the year, I drove to Chilmark in the darkness, a light mist on my windshield, the remnants of a shower that weather forecasts said would soon cease. My plan, worked out over hours of mental tumbling, was to find a good spot to sit on the downwind side of a shallow, relatively unobstructed ravine that ran north-south and appeared to provide a good route for deer moving to and from bedding areas.

As I prepared to leave my truck, I considered bringing along my modern scoped muzzleloader, in the event I saw a deer at some distance. Committed to my plan, I quickly discounted the idea.

I had a short walk along a dirt road in the lifting darkness and then walked along a path that entered a break in a stone wall. I paused. The wall overlooked a saddle I knew the deer sometimes used. So often in fishing and hunting we second-guess ourselves. "Stick with the plan," I told myself.

I walked up the side of the ravine and found a large, gnarly, well-branched oak that provided a perfect vantage point and gun rest. Then I waited.

Several weeks ago, I read a gun-control opinion piece published in the New York Times (Dec. 19, "The Deer in My Sights,") by Seamus McGraw, in which he described stalking a deer for more than an hour in the Pennsylvania woods with his 50-caliber flint-lock, only to get within 30 feet of it — a hard-to-believe scenario for anyone who has tried to walk within even 100 yards of a deer, let alone 30 feet — only to put his weapon down and clap his hands to send the deer scurrying into the woods.

"The simple fact was that I was too poisoned by bitterness to use my weapon honorably," he said, referring to recent news reports detailing violence around the nation and his disdain for "Second Amendment extremists in the upper echelons of the National Rifle Association and in Congress who have no clue what the real purpose of a gun is."

I was untroubled by such thoughts on the last day of the season. If a deer walked within 30 feet or 30 yards of me, I planned to shoot it. Not because I was less sensitive than Seamus (well, maybe by New York Times standards), but because I think the gun debate has little to do with hunting and much to do with differing American cultures and the willingness of good people on all sides to talk past each other.

My thoughts that morning were focused on the ground in front of me as fog rolled through the trees. The snap of a twig drew my attention to my left, where a large doe was walking up the ravine.

I watched as she started to move leisurely up the other side of the ravine, walking away from me.

According to Mr. Ambrose, Captain Lewis was an excellent shot, particularly when using his walking stick as a rifle rest: "If the target was within a hundred yards and bigger than a mouse, he usually got it."

I had a large branch in place of a walking stick, and knew I would be hard-pressed to hit a barn door at 100 yards.

The doe was about 70 yards away. I rested the rifle on the branch, centered the metal sights on the deer and pulled the trigger: There was a loud click as the flint struck the frizzen but no bang. Not good.

The deer looked in my direction, alert, ears and tail twitching, sniffing the air. I had the advantage of the wind, a critical factor when hunting deer, which possess an acute sense of smell.

I quickly wiped the damp powder from the flash pan and added a fresh charge of priming powder. The doe resumed feeding in a new direction that brought her closer to me. She was about 40 yards away as I tried to calm my excited breathing in preparation for pulling the trigger.

I fired. The deer fell on the spot. It pays to stick with the plan.

Ducks, Geese, Pheasants and Turkeys

Tisbury Pond Club members, 1913

"Oh Lord, from error's ways defend us, Lest we mistake thy will for luck.

Give us at dawn, a flight stupendous, Don't send us coot, but geese and ducks."

The Tisbury Pond Club "Duck Grace" was to be said by the assembled members of the club and their guests "prior to the evening repast on each day of the week, except that on Saturdays, being the day next preceding the Lord's Day, the grace shall be omitted."

Labs Doing What They're Bred to Do

You can't put a price on a good dog.
(January 1998)

TASHMOO, MY TWO-YEAR-OLD Labrador retriever, waited at the door for me, his tail wagging like a dog metronome, an indicator of all the excitement and enthusiasm his breed can muster — which is considerable — for one last morning retrieving ducks in the icy water.

Even a few weeks into the season he had needed no prodding, just a quiet whisper, to rise from his cushion in the basement where he lay comfortably asleep. He shook his head quickly in a wake-up ritual that made his jowls and ears flap from side to side with a distinctive sound of "whoppa, whoppa, whoppa." Seeing a shotgun leaning by the wall brought him to the kitchen door where he kept turning his head in my direction with a look of anticipation as if to say, "Let's get going."

Both of us were new to the sport, and while we had gone out a few times last year, the joy of duck hunting was something we had discovered together this season. Now, with only one week left, like a fine banquet, both of us were reluctant to see it end. Most of all, I did not know how I would explain it to Tashmoo when he stood by the door with an expectant gaze.

Not that I would miss leaving my bed well before the sun rose. But there had been something special about watching a dog do

Emmett (left) and Tashmoo sit as decoys
are gathered in a pile following a morning
duck hunt on Tisbury Great Pond.

something that every instinct told him it was born to do, and I
would miss that over the coming months.

Tashmoo was not born with a well-documented and expensive
pedigree. He was a $50 Chilmark Lab, the product of an uncompli-
cated and casual up-Island summer romance. But, like the noblest
to the most humble Labrador retriever, he was heir to every gene
that ever imparted the notion that there is sheer joy in plunging
into the cold water to fetch a duck, or for the less genetically dis-
posed Lab, to scour a bedroom for a sock or shoe.

On one occasion when he completed a double retrieve, despite
the lack of any real training on my part, I beamed with pride like a
proud parent whose child has exceeded his expectations.

"Not bad for a fifty dollar dog," I said to Cooper Gilkes, my
frequent hunting partner.

Coop, an expert in most outdoor pursuits, had attempted to
teach both dog and master the finer points of duck hunting. It did
not take Tashmoo many mornings to discover who was the better
marksman. Left unfettered he would divide his time sitting beside
me, then Coop. I tried not to take it personally.

It takes a certain motivation to rise early on a "good" day for duck hunting, which usually means wind and rain. But even on those mornings when the wind blows wet and cold out of the gray northeast, there is an elemental beauty in the Vineyard's shore and marshes, and in the sight of a Lab swimming, its powerful chest pushing the water aside. That is as much a part of the world of duck hunting as a finely made shot and may help explain why someone sets out in the dark morning hours which distinguish duck hunting from more comfortable pursuits.

On a number of mornings we hunted with my friend Alley Moore and his dog, Emmett, an 18-month-old black Lab. The dogs had become fast friends after an initial meeting early in the season that began with one growl and much lifting of legs and ended with them running, rolling, and tumbling around like long-lost brothers.

A flight of mergansers, sea ducks, passed overhead on our last day of hunting, a perfect morning of shooting along Tisbury Great Pond. Two well-aimed shots sent two birds crashing into the water, followed quickly by Emmett and Tashmoo. Both dogs returned to shore holding their limp quarry softly in their mouths with an unmistakable look of accomplishment and joy.

It will be another nine months before we would hunt ducks again. A long time in dog years.

When Bad Shots Happen
to Good Dogs

A hunting dog's faith may be tested but never wavers.
(December 1998)

A DOG BORN WITH the instinct to retrieve expects his master to hit the mark. I knew that by the look Tashmoo gave me one morning as my shots echoed in quick succession over a saltmarsh pothole from which mallards and black ducks had lifted and hung like Christmas ornaments in the air over my head, but no ducks fell.

We both lacked a certain hunting pedigree when my friend and all-around Island sportsman Cooper Gilkes introduced both of us to the Island's waterfowling legacy a few years ago. The closest I had ever come to duck hunting growing up in Boston was trying to kick a pigeon on Boston Common. And the only papers Tashmoo, a black Labrador retriever, had when I bought him for $50 were spread out under him and his siblings in Chilmark.

But Tashmoo was born with the genetic promptings that tell a Lab that life is fun, and nothing is more fun than plunging into the cold water to bring back a duck or flush a pheasant from out of a tangle of briars and thorns. Unfortunately, I could not call on any natural skills, no hand-eye coordination passed down through my family tree. Still, I looked forward to the arrival of this hunting season confident that with a few years of limited experience I could at least tell an eider from a black duck and that my shooting had marginally improved. That confidence was short-lived.

Each fall, the state Division of Fisheries and Wildlife stocks pheasants in the Manuel F. Correllus State Forest located in the middle of the Island. One afternoon, I combined a walk with pheasant hunting. I was carrying a 12-gauge shotgun, but the truth is I did not expect to see a thing and was not paying attention when, three minutes into our walk, Tashmoo put his nose into a clump of brush at the edge of a field, his tail a metronome marking his level of excitement.

Suddenly, a pheasant erupted in flight.

Boom. Boom. Boom. Three shots. Three misses. The bird flew along the edge of thick pines and disappeared into the woods. Tashmoo bounced ahead.

"Come on back Tash," I yelled after him, embarrassed by his faith in me and my lack of faith in him. "I missed it."

I looked for redemption one morning as we sat at the edge of a farm field in Katama waiting for geese to fly. I had a goose call Coop had left with me. I was new to the technique and except for striking a few notes that imitated the sound of an ill buzzard, I was doing pretty well.

The sun was just climbing up over the horizon as I tooted away, half-awake and not as alert as a duck hunter should be if he does not want to squander the morning minutes. Tashmoo, though, had his gaze firmly set. I looked away to the west so the sun would not be in my eyes. I turned back to see a flight of geese gliding over the decoys set out right in front of me. I brought the shotgun to my shoulder and fired once as they flew away and out of the field.

Tashmoo looked up at me with an expression that said, "Well?"

"I won't say anything if you don't," I said.

I was beginning to be depressed. My dog deserved better than flubbed opportunities. One morning I sat below the crest of a dune on Chappaquiddick with Ralph Case of Edgartown and never fired my gun at all, content to sit and watch. With one shot Ralph brought down two coot, sea ducks that come in fast and low from the ocean. Tashmoo retrieved ducks all morning that he tried to pass off to me instead of Ralph.

I knew I had a good dog and I was a bad shot. I was determined to improve.

It was the last week of pheasant season. Alley Moore, his lab Emmett, Tashmoo, and I had walked the fields of Katama for an hour. We were nearing the car and the end of our hunt when Tashmoo and Emmett picked up a scent. Their tails started their excited beat. I watched Tashmoo carefully as he probed the brush.

A pheasant burst up. I took careful aim and dropped it with one shot into thick briars. Undeterred Tashmoo went into the tangled underbrush and returned with our quarry.

On the Pheasant Trail, a Good Working Dog Is a Fine Companion

(November 1999)

THE PHEASANT SEASON began in mid-October on the last day of the striped bass and bluefish derby. If dogs kept calendars, I am certain that Tashmoo, my five-year-old Labrador retriever, would have circled that date.

Fishing season is not much fun for my dog. Despite the imploring Lab look I get when I stand at the door with my fishing rod in hand, any interest in having Tashmoo for company on the beach disappeared a few years ago when he decided to mix it up with a skunk as I was battling a striper.

For much of the year, Tashmoo's daily routine pretty much consists of lying about our small house at various spots on the floor and rug. He picks his resting places based on the position of the sun's rays and other criteria I can only guess at.

But that all changes with the start of the bird hunting season. This is his time, and he knows it. By the second day of the pheasant season, I had only to grab my new hunting boots from Cabela's, the giant Midwestern mail order outfitter (most comfortable pair of boots I ever put on out of the box), and Tashmoo would be sitting by the door, tail wagging furiously.

Unlike duck hunting on the Vineyard, the six-week pheasant season is an artificial product. It relies on stockings by the state Division of Fisheries and Wildlife (DFW) to create any real hunting opportunities on lands accessible by the general public, principally in the Manuel F. Corellus State Forest and Katama Farm plains.

What there is of an indigenous population of wild birds on the Island pretty much sticks to private farm lands, fields, and grasslands. Those pheasants are hardy survivors. Like all of the Vineyard's ground-nesting birds, their population survives despite a host of predators that includes hawks, owls, feral cats, skunks, and raccoons.

Hunting pheasants on the Vineyard will never rival a cornfield in Nebraska. But there is still a sense of anticipation for the hunter who takes a walk with a dog with a good nose on a crisp fall day and holds a shotgun in the crook of his arm.

According to a story in the Wall Street Journal published Feb. 1, 1999, the first effort to introduce pheasants into the United States was made by Richard Bache, the son-in-law of Benjamin Franklin. He brought over English blacknecks from England in the late 1700s, apparently without much success. Approximately 100 years later, Judge Owen Denny of Oregon received a diplomatic appointment from President Ulysses Grant to Shanghai, where he tasted ringneck pheasant for the first time.

Impressed with the game and culinary qualities of the ringneck, in 1881 and again in 1882 Judge Denny shipped a small number of birds to his brother's farm in Oregon and asked area "shootists" to let the birds become established. By 1892 a reported 50,000 cocks were killed on opening day of Oregon's first pheasant season.

As settlers continued to move west, clearing fields and growing crops, Judge Denny's Chinese ringnecks moved east and were augmented by semi-domesticated English stocks. Pheasants spread across the nation, quickly adapting to the vast agricultural areas of the Midwest and the brushy cover adjacent to New England farm fields. In many areas of the country, the pheasant provided hunters at all levels of society and from every background with a bird they could hunt without traveling very far.

But development, loss of habitat, and increased pesticide use have affected pheasant numbers over the past decades. In many parts of the country, hunters must now rely on private clubs or preserves to enjoy a day of hunting. Some clubs require hefty fees and have all the amenities of a fancy country club. Others have more basic arrangements based on a simple sharing of costs to lease and stock a sufficient parcel of land where members are allowed to hunt.

The state stocking program is funded entirely by the sale of hunting licenses. A friend jokingly calls the program, "pheasants for peasants," but it ensures that even hunters without access to private property or special privileges can enjoy the excitement of hunting pheasants in the field.

Dick Burrell, DFW game biologist, says the state buys approximately 40,000 birds a year from six vendors. The Vineyard is stocked twice a season, once at the beginning and again at midpoint, while some places on the Cape are stocked as often as three times a week. Mr. Burrell says that logistical problems limit the number of times birds can be sent to the Vineyard. Because the Island sustains a natural population of birds, the state stocks only cocks, not hens, to protect as much as possible the wild strain.

Grasslands, coastal sand plains, farmland, and early successional fields all provide good habitat for pheasants. But development and the spread of woodlands all limit the amount of area that can sustain a natural population. Changing cultivation practices also play a role. In just one small example, Katama Farm no longer grows the stands of corn that once provided cover and food for a variety of birds, including pheasants.

Last month, the Wampanoag Tribe's natural resource department released 115 cocks and 100 hens on tribal land in Aquinnah as part of an effort to create a standing population of pheasants. The stocking took place in conjunction with a continuing effort to control the population of skunks and raccoons.

Bret Stearns, tribal natural resource officer, says the birds have dispersed well but have become a target for hawks and other predators. All the birds are banded, but none have yet been shot by tribal hunters.

Organizations such as Pheasants Forever, a Minnesota-based conservation organization dedicated to increasing pheasant habitat, emphasizes habitat restoration and transplanting of wild pheasants as opposed to the stocking of less predator-wary pen-raised birds, which the group says is an ineffective method of re-establishing natural populations. But Mr. Stearns says the tribe is keeping close track of all the birds and will reassess the program based on its results. Time will tell if the tribe's restocking efforts will produce dividends for the entire Island.

Hunting pheasant does not absolutely require a dog, but it enriches the experience immensely. When a dog is on his or her game, the shot that takes the bird is only the culmination, not the point of the hunt.

Early in the season, Tashmoo and I had covered a considerable distance in the State Forest, walking around the perimeter of a large, open field, when he suddenly stopped and thrust his nose into the air, black nostrils pumping furiously. One scent in the swirling currents of wind blowing through the thickets and brush had caught his attention.

Lowering his head to the ground, he raced in one direction then the other, abruptly shifting his route as he followed an unseen olfactory trail hanging in the air. A stiff wind made the job harder but did little to diminish his ardor. Minute after minute he raced one way then the other, circling, stopping to hold his nose in the air, then circling again. I watched until he ran headlong into a thicket of scrub oak and brush.

With a loud cackle, a bright cock pheasant erupted from its hiding place. I brought my Remington 12-gauge to my shoulder, reminding myself to lead the bird, and fired once.

Later that night, I joined some friends fishing the bottom along the South Shore for late season striped bass. Sitting back under the stars waiting for a rod to bend under the weight of a fish, it occurred to me that some of those same people who see rural quality in a new architecturally designed wooden firehouse are just as quick to cast a disparaging glance when they encounter a hunter in a Vineyard field with a dog.

I don't know how they define rural quality in the heartland of Nebraska, but I do know that no cornhusker ever began his day chasing pheasants in the morning and ended it catching striped bass at night in the rolling salt surf.

Hunting's Rich Tradition Is Chronicled in Tisbury Pond Club's Journal

More than one century ago, duck hunters sang in praise of Mrs. Slocum's apple pie and a flight of geese and ducks.
(November 2000)

THE SUN WAS still beneath the eastern horizon of Long Point as the sound of a waterfowler's shotgun reverberated in the distance on Tisbury Great Pond Thanksgiving morning.

Tashmoo's ears perked up in anticipation. I was glad the shots were some distance away. Despite his unquestioned loyalty, my Lab's unbridled enthusiasm for fetching ducks sometimes overpowers his training, and he has been known to run off anxious to offer a nearby gunner a helping retrieve.

The wind was cold and strong from the northwest. The evening forecast had called for snow squalls, but the first day of the winter duck season dawned clear and few birds were flying, evidently content to remain where they had spent the night. Despite Martha's Vineyard's rich waterfowling tradition, it is increasingly difficult to find a spot on one of the Island's salt ponds from which to hunt. New, luxurious homes rise up from the landscape, a testament to this generation's prosperity.

Still, sitting in a makeshift blind with a small spread of mallard and black duck cork decoys bobbing on the water, it is possible to imagine the distant echoes of long still guns. And remember another era of national wealth almost a century ago when it was enough to have a simple camp, a good dog, and "a flight stupendous."

The Tisbury Pond Club

The Long Point Wildlife Refuge, 633 acres of woods, salt marsh, pond, and barrier beach overlooking Tisbury Great Pond and the Atlantic Ocean is owned and managed by The Trustees of Reservations (TTOR). According to the informative "Land Use History of Long Point," a 30-page work by Lloyd Raleigh, TTOR regional ecologist, in the early part of the 20th century wealthy industrialists set up hunting clubs along the Island's south shore. The Watcha Club, set up in 1903, was the first in the Long Point area, followed by the Tisbury Pond Club in 1912 with the club's initial purchase of 470 acres. By 1930 the entire area between Tisbury Great Pond and Oyster Pond was owned or controlled by hunting clubs.

The history of the Tisbury Pond Club is recorded in a journal purchased from Hooper, Lewis & Co, stationers on Federal Street in Boston, and embossed with the words, "Tisbury Pond Club, 1912, Martha's Vineyard." The first handwritten entry on a now yellowing page reports: "The formation of the club was first considered in the spring of 1912, and after the property was purchased, John K. Burgess was put in charge of fitting and furnishing, and made a number of trips to Tisbury for those purposes."
It is also noted that, "The first use of the clubhouse by a party of members was on Sept. 24. G.T. Rice, T.F. Baxter, J. Crane and the latter's two guests, W.S. Crane and Emery Crane, went down on the 1.25 train, arrived at the club just after dark, due to going to Oak Bluffs instead of Vineyard Haven. Mrs. Joshua Slocum

and Capt. Cleveland welcomed us. Few black ducks about and a few shore birds. Cleveland had shot three blacks, which were cooked for supper. Wind strong easterly, cloudy."

Club member J. Crane and dog, Julia.

Located in a TTOR office a few years ago, the journal includes notes on each day's hunt from the years 1912 to 1919 and faded photographs of club members, the clubhouse, and its surroundings. Spare and to the point, the day's tally and weather was noted in the neat cursive handwriting style of the day.

For example, Saturday, Oct. 12, 1912, "In afternoon W.B. Rogers, J.K. Burgess and G.T. Rice took blinds on east side of point. Mild and light air. One black and one widgeon by W.B.R. both coming from eastward."

Shooting was better on Saturday, Dec. 7, with a strong west wind. On that day the members took a catboat across the pond and bagged a total of 26 birds including 7 redheads, 8 bluebills, and 2 widgeon.

By year's end the tally would be 185 birds, or 5 birds per shooting day, as noted in the journal which listed the season's bag for each year. The most number of birds shot, 423, was in 1914. The least, 27, was in 1918. A notation in the margin for the years 1917, 1918, and 1919 says simply: war.

Mrs. Slocum's Apple Pie

In the early years of the clubs, live geese were often kept as decoys. The clubhouse, decoys, and blinds the members shot from were maintained by a series of Island caretakers with familiar Island names.

Social distinctions were more obvious and accepted when the Vineyard first came into its own as a vacation retreat from the city. But there was an obvious affection and friendship between the club members and the Islanders they depended on for their needs.

According to the TTOR history, one caretaker, Marshall Norton, listened to the members of the club when they talked about stocks and purchased the same stocks. Eventually, he was able to purchase 80 acres with his capital gains.

The apple pies baked by Mrs. Slocum inspired one club member, Dwight Blany, to write a song. The three verses are included in the journal with the note that it should be sung to the tune of "The Yellow Rose of Texas."

I've travelled the world over,
and shot from many blinds,
I've often fed on clover,
And pie of many kinds.
Tho' milk I do not care for
Nor honey of the bee
It is Mrs. Slocum's apple pie
That's all the world to me."

Some call out loud for lobster
For flapjacks some do yell
And some for roasted turkey
Will wildly ring the bell.
But give me Martha's Vineyard
From Gay Head to Tisburee
And Mrs. Slocum's apple pie
Is all the world to me

Oh I'm going back to Eastham,
To my dogs and ducks and guns.
Where we live on quahaug chowder,
On oysters, fish and buns.
But my heart is sad and lonely,
For my home I'd like to see.
Though Mrs. Slocum's apple pie,
Is all the world to me.

The simple wooden building that once served as the clubhouse for the Tisbury Pond Club appears almost out of place when compared with a new more architecturally distinctive residence just across Middle Cove. Now an office and residence for TTOR, from the porch it is possible to scan the sky over Tisbury Great Pond and Long Pond in search of ducks.

In 1979 the Long Point property enjoyed by thousands of Island residents and visitors each year was given to the trustees by Frederick Blodgett, Carl Gilbert, and William Rogers, the three remaining members of the Tisbury Pond Club.

In a conversation before he died in 1999, Mr. Blodgett, then 95 years old, said that despite offers of a great deal of money he and the remaining club members wanted to ensure that the property would be "forever for the public and would never be developed."

Chris Kennedy, TTOR islands regional director, said many people do not realize that sportsmen were some of the country's first conservationists. He said without the generosity and vision of the club members it is unlikely the property would exist as it does today.

Mr. Kennedy said, "If it had not been for that rich hunting tradition, we can't say it would not have been another development."

Mr. Kennedy added, "It strikes you immediately when you read the log book, you are looking at a different time, a different view point, where hunting was an accepted part of life."

He said a large part of that life was the camaraderie of the clubhouse, which remained a simple structure. Mr. Kennedy observed, "They didn't come to Long Point to make it part of Boston."

Two Island waterfowlers.

Chris Eagan, TTOR Long Point refuge manager, said that standing in the paneled rooms of the clubhouse, it is still possible to get a sense of the atmosphere that once prevailed as the men relaxed after a day in the blinds, drinking whiskey and smoking cigars.

A sheet of paper tucked into the journal includes the "Duck Grace," which was to be said by the assembled members of the club and their guests "prior to the evening repast on each day of the week, except that on Saturdays, being the day next preceding the Lord's Day, the grace shall be omitted."

As any waterfowler knows, all ducks are not created equal when it comes to the dinner table, and the gunners of the Tisbury Pond Club recognized the failings of coot, a seabird, in their prayer:

"Oh Lord, from error's ways defend us, Lest we mistake thy will for luck. Give us at dawn, a flight stupendous, Don't send us coot, but geese and ducks."

According to Mr. Eagan, many of the old photos that still hang on the walls of the clubhouse will one day be housed in the new Long Point visitor's center. Mr. Eagan said the fact that Long Point even exists as it does is a testament to the vision of the club members.

Anticipating my first day's hunt, I looked at the entry for Thanksgiving Day, 1912. The club member who recorded that day's shooting wrote, "Good shooting, though birds were rather high. Strong north wind and snow. Gale at night shifting to N.W. early in morning. Fourteen birds, one black, two redheads, eleven bluebills."

The morning forecast called for snow squalls as I eagerly prepared my decoys and gear. My wife looked on with amusement at the idea that I was "spending all this time to get ready and go shoot at ducks that nobody wants to eat."

A little later she interrupted my preparations to announce that it was 28 degrees out. For good measure, she added the news that the temperature on Mount Washington was minus two.

It is hard to explain the attraction of rising before dawn to sit on the shore of Tisbury Great Pond and scan the sky for ducks. But listening to the distant echoes of shotguns in the air, I was sure the members of the Tisbury Pond Club would have understood.

Goose Sausage Proves to be Good Stuff

A handy machine answered the vexing question of how to convert geese into tasty table fare.
(October 2015)

THE LARGE FLOCK of geese continued to swim up the cove as I crouched behind a pile of brush fashioned into a blind overlooking Tisbury Great Pond Saturday morning, my ancient Browning humpback shotgun at the ready, as I anticipated the moment when the birds would take flight and, if all went as I expected, fly past my hunting companion Alley Moore and me.

The geese continued to talk to one another, their pace of calling quickening. Perhaps, absent air traffic controllers, they all have to agree when it is time to lift off.

Honk — What do you think? Honk — Looks good to me. Honk — Should we wait? Honk — What about that field we went to yesterday? Honk — See those guys over there? Honk — What guys?

With one final round of excited honks, the flock of geese lifted off the water, gaining speed and altitude. I shot once but made a critical error — I looked at all the geese, instead of focusing on one goose, and did not bring down a bird. I know better, and mentally berated myself.

Otis looked disappointed, but quickly got over it, as black Labs do — it is a breed that does not bear a grudge — and he began scanning the sky, optimistic that his owner, Alley, and I would not fail him when the next group of geese flew by us on the last day of the early regular duck season. A short time later, we redeemed his faith.

I never squeeze the trigger of my Browning shotgun with its well-beat-up stock without thinking of builder, lobsterman, decoy carver, and longtime quintessential Yankee selectman, Herbert Hancock of Chilmark. Herb shot plenty of ducks, geese, and deer with that beat-up weapon, already an old gun when he handed it to me unceremoniously just weeks before his death in April 2001. I suspect he is pleased it is still being used to take the odd goose or duck, and I am equally pleased to be its owner.

The legendary American gun designer John Browning's genius is evident in this aged 12-gauge shotgun, which continues to operate flawlessly. Production of the Browning Auto-5, the first mass-produced semiautomatic shotgun, began in 1902 and ended in 1999. Not a bad run.

I had two geese in hand. Ordinarily, I would have been thinking about who might be willing to take the birds. Wild goose has never been a favorite of mine, despite numerous attempts to find a good recipe.

Years ago I plucked a whole bird for a holiday dinner. I turned the oven into a greasy, sooty mess, and ended up with a dry, tough bird that reminded me of overdone roast beef. Cooking a goose breast on the grill was hit or miss, mostly miss.

When I have time, I like to turn my tougher cuts of venison into sausage. I figured I could do the same with the goose breasts. The September early goose season provided an opportunity to experiment.

The very helpful butchers at Reliable Market in Oak Bluffs provided me with casings, sweet Italian seasonings, pork trimming, and pork fat. The final product was delicious. The sausage process, however, was a chore.

The meat-grinding attachment on our KitchenAid mixer worked fine. The sausage-stuffer attachment was another story. The ground meat barely moved through the tube.

Sausage making takes an extra set of hands, and in my case that meant my wife Norma, whom I instructed to funnel the meat faster or slower and generally held responsible for the sausage casing hernias that continually developed. That she did not chuck a goose meatball at me was a testament to her patience. I knew there was something wrong, and assumed it was us or the consistency of the mixture. Time for a Google search. The amazing thing, at least to me, is I can type in a question such as, "Why can't I stuff sausage with my KitchenAid mixer?" and I actually find several answers. People have pondered the question.

The problem was not Norma and me, but our useless stuffer attachment. A little more research turned up LEM, a company that bills itself as "the leader in game processing."

A few weeks ago, Norma and I made a quick stop at Bass Pro Shop in Foxborough, where I purchased a LEM vertical sausage stuffer with a five-pound capacity. On Sunday I decided to put it to good use.

The four goose breasts, trimmed of any wounds, produced three pounds of meat. I added one pound of pork butt and one pound of pork fat, and the called-for amount of LEM sweet Italian sausage seasoning. The moment of truth came when Norma started cranking the handle of the sausage stuffer, which acts like a giant sausage syringe. The meat flowed effortlessly through the tube. Honk. Honk.

Don't Brake for Turkeys

Motorists who let turkeys cross the road as though they were kids in a crosswalk send the wrong message to the tasty feather dusters. (April 2016)

MARTHA'S VINEYARD IS fortunate to have flocks of turkeys; they are grand animals to look at, particularly a tom strutting his stuff in full feathered regalia. However, well-meaning people who treat the official wild game bird of Massachusetts like a parolee from a Thanksgiving dinner granted a new lease on life do these birds no favors.

I get exasperated whenever I am driving along Franklin Street in Vineyard Haven, a notorious turkey hangout, and a driver comes to a complete halt to allow the members of a flock, one by one, to pass, rather than proceeding slowly. "No, don't stop," I shout in frustration at the lesson being imprinted on those little turkey brains: Cars and trucks will stop for us — not always.

Massachusetts Division of Fisheries and Wildlife (DFW) biologists stress that turkeys are wild animals and should be treated as such. Nothing drives home that point to a turkey like getting shot at during the state's fall or spring hunting season, which began Monday and ends May 21. But for a variety of reasons, Island hunters generally pass up the opportunity to take a turkey, and so miss out on delicious table fare.

A pair of toms strut in the front yard of a Vineyard
Haven home off Franklin Street.

Other than during the spring mating season, turkeys are all about finding food. As a result, many of the Island's birds take up permanent residence in neighborhoods where they are fed and unmolested by humans whom, for all their kindness, the turkey may place at the bottom of its pecking order.

Pampering any wild animal — feeding it, sheltering it, or treating it as a pet — is ultimately harmful to wildlife, DFW biologists stress. In the short term for a turkey, perhaps not as harmful as getting hit by a 12-gauge load of No. 5 shot, but certainly in the long term.

Each hen lays from 12 to 15 eggs. Not all survive, but with few natural predators, turkey numbers will continue to increase. Our growing turkey population may one day move from the category of wildlife to unwholesome pests, much like geese, which once migrated south, but now reside on the Island year-round, fouling our fields, polluting our waterways, and damaging farmlands.

The Island population of turkeys may be the descendants of turkey stock raised on game farms and brought to the Vineyard, but no one is certain. They have characteristics of wild Eastern birds, DFW turkey and upland game biologist Dave Scarpitti told me. "It's a unique thing," he said.

At the time of colonial settlement, the wild turkey was widespread in Massachusetts, ranging from Cape Cod to the Berkshires, according to the DFW website. As settlement progressed, however, hardwood forests were cut and the range of the turkey began to shrink. By the early 1800s turkeys were rare in the state, and the last known native bird was killed on Mount Tom in 1851.

By the early 1900s, it appeared the turkey might go extinct. The nation's population stood at about 30,000, a result of habitat loss and overhunting. Just as with deer, elk, and ducks, hunter conservationists and hunter dollars are widely responsible for bringing the turkey back. Founded in 1973, the National Wild Turkey Federation (NWTF) is emblematic of the effort. The nonprofit has invested $488 million in wildlife conservation and the preservation of our hunting heritage, and improved more than 17 million acres of wildlife habitat, benefiting hunters and non-hunters alike.

There are now nearly seven million wild turkeys in every state but Alaska. Following several failed attempts in the '60s, wild birds were successfully reintroduced in Massachusetts in the '70s, beginning with Beartown State Forest in southern Berkshire County.

Across much of the turkey's range, the bird that Benjamin Franklin thought best deserved to be our nation's symbol is no easy quarry — and turkey hunting generates the same kind of passion fishing season does on the Vineyard. A 2006 federal report estimated that nationally turkey hunters spent $1.5 billion annually on turkey hunting (that includes gas, hotels, equipment, etc). And the number of turkey hunters continues to grow — from 2.6 million turkey hunters in 2006 to 3.1 million in 2011.

In a telephone call from NWTF headquarters in Edgefield, S.C., Tom Hughes, a wildlife biologist and assistant vice president of science and technology, described the hold of turkey hunting. By way of introduction, Tom told me, "I have been hunting turkeys pretty hard since 1978, not missing a season in there, and not missing more days than I can help, so I've been a convert for quite some time; let's put it that way."

Tom said it is the challenge, and that begins with the nature of turkey vocalizations during the spring mating season. The male gobbles to attract the hens, and the hen yelps in response. In nature, the hen goes to the tom. The challenge the hunter faces is to get the tom to come to him, and within shooting range. True wild turkeys are extremely cautious, and very sensitive to any movement. "They have incredible eyesight, and if you move while their head's in the open, they will see you, you can just count on it," Tom said.

"The chess match nature of all this is what appeals to me," he said. "You try to get close enough to the gobbler that you can get his attention, not so close that he'll see you, and you try to call just enough to get him interested but not so much that he gets suspicious or not so little that he's not interested ... Just the thrill of hearing a wild turkey gobble and call back to you, and you being good enough to close the deal and make it all work out — that has always appealed to me."

Not much strategy is needed on Martha's Vineyard. I had not previously hunted turkeys, in part because the fall and spring turkey seasons coincided with other interests, such as fish, deer, and ducks. But I was always interested in the table qualities of a wild turkey. I imagined the meat to be quite dark and tough; I was wrong on both counts.

Last May, a friend, an experienced turkey hunter who does most of his turkey hunting in New York State, where the birds know better than to hang around humans, indulged me with a turkey hunt in the wilds of Chilmark. I met him before dawn, and we walked into the woods until we found a spot where he expected the turkeys, still roosting high in a grove of nearby trees, would pass. He began to call, and the gobblers called back, whether to us I really don't know. I do know that one gobbler's lack of concern when he walked by me and I raised my shotgun was a fatal mistake.

I set the turkey breasts in a brine solution, then put them in my Masterbuilt electric smoker for about two hours. The result was beyond my expectations, and much tastier than anything I had ever purchased at a meat counter. My wife and I dined on the best turkey sandwiches we had ever eaten.

The DFW website provides some informative information on how to prevent conflicts with wild turkeys. It advises against allowing turkeys to become habituated to people, and notes that "humans perceived as males may be threatened or challenged by adult gobblers, especially in spring, or may be followed and called at by hens."

If having a turkey come on to you sexually is not alarming enough, consider that a turkey may put you at the bottom of its pecking order, and try to bully you.

Off Island

A Bajan fisherman makes a flawless throw of a cast
net over a pod of baitfish.

*Colvin was bottom-fishing near a rocky point for anything he could catch
to eat. His tackle consisted of two broken spinning reels, one of which he
jammed with a piece of wood to keep it from revolving freely, and heavy surf
rods with broken guides. ... I handed him several lures, including some
Deadly Dicks, and a Martha's Vineyard Bass and Bluefish Derby fishing
cap. I told him about our Island's annual fishing tournament — the cen-
terpiece of so many Island friendships. Colvin was genuinely happy about
his new hat and his new friend, as was I.*

Island Hunters Find Fun,
Friends in Alabama

For a pair of visiting Yankees, Union Springs was not exactly King Arthur's Court.
(February 2010)

BUCK IS A big yellow dog with a character flaw. He would, when presented with the opportunity, eat a cat. All the guests seated in Jim and Jane Klingler's elegant dining room one recent evening as the Klinglers entertained two visitors from Martha's Vineyard were willing to overlook those transgressions.

"Buck's a good dog," Heather Klinck of West Tisbury and Union Springs, Alabama said, as Jane and Jim told the story of how they had discovered that Buck could not be trusted around felines.

And all agreed that the visit of the Klinglers' daughter and grandkids with their new kitten, which led to the discovery of Buck's character flaw, was unfortunate. However, it was quickly smoothed over when grandma invited the kids into the kitchen to bake cookies.

After all, Buck had shown himself to be fearless when Jim shot a coyote he spotted from his back door and had to track it down. And Buck proved to be good at keeping deer out of the yard. The Klingler partnership with Buck was a no-frills relationship. Buck, "a big yella dog" adopted from the pound, slept outside on a mat by the back door and stayed there, where he kept an eye on the property, and in return for his devotion, the Klinglers loved him and overlooked an occasional transgression.

Buck enjoys some attention from Coop.

"Uh huh," Jimmy Bassett, a banker turned co-owner of Beck's turf supply company, agreed from across the table. "He's a good dog," he said in the soft drawn out tones of a native Alabamian.

It was a compliment of the highest order in the community of Bullock County, where people respect and value good dogs, family, friends, country, religious bonds, steady horses, accurate rifles, fast quail, homebrewed whiskey, turkey hunting, deer hunting, and Alabama football — in an order of preference and passion that depends on the individual.

Cooper Gilkes of Edgartown and I visited Union Springs last month to go quail hunting, at the invitation of Charles and Heather Klinck. It seemed a fine way to help bridge the gap between the end of the Island's deer and duck hunting seasons and the arrival of striped bass in the spring.

It was also an opportunity to experience southern hospitality and to be reminded that every now and then it is healthy to leave reverential, self-congratulatory Martha's Vineyard and discover the richness elsewhere in America.

Over the course of our week-long trip, I learned that I never want to drive through the city of Atlanta again, where the prevailing speed limit is 85 miles per hour and lane changing is a sport; that the secret to making grits is "low and slow"; that a coon ass is a Cajun from Louisiana, but it is best to smile when you call him that; that a Remington 700 rifle and Winchester 308 cartridge is a deadly combination for hunting deer; and that Coop should work for the CIA, because I would take waterboarding any day over sharing a room with him when he begins to snore.

In the summer, the Klincks enjoy boating and entertaining friends on Martha's Vineyard. Heather grew up in Colorado, but was a regular Island visitor. Her aunt, the artist Rose Abrahamson, has always lived on the Vineyard. Later, her parents, Stanley and Adele Schonbrun retired to West Tisbury.

Charles, who retains the distinctive drawl of his hometown of Jackson, Mississippi, met Heather in his home state, where she attended college. A lifelong hunter, Charles introduced Heather to the world of bird dogs. It is a passion that led them to build a house 10 years ago in Union Springs, a small, rural town south of Montgomery, proclaimed to be "the bird dog field trial capital of the world."

It is a boast underscored by a life-size bronze statue of an English pointer on a granite pillar inscribed with the names of men and women who have contributed to the sport of field trialing. The statue is located smack in the middle of Prairie Street, just down from the Bullock County courthouse and the Fair Company department store, where the fashions and mannequins, frozen in time behind a pair of locked glass doors, have skipped decades of passing styles.

Martha's Vineyard has plenty of quirky stories, but try this one on for size. Zelda and James Mahaffey worked in the small-town department store they owned for years and years. Mr. Mahaffey wanted to go on vacation, but his wife did not. One day, Mr. Mahaffey convinced his wife to close Fair Company for one week.

"She had so much fun she decided not to reopen," Heather told me as I peered through the glass door at racks of clothing with price tags dating to the 1980s. And there the store sits with curls of white paint peeling from the ceiling over fashions a retro rocker would die for.

The population of Union Springs is 3,670. The median house value is $57,800, and the median age 31, according to the town's website.

There is a one-reporter local newspaper, the Union Springs Herald, circulation 3,100. The reporter is Jovani Yolanda Fox, an enthusiastic young journalism graduate from Boston who returned to her family roots and does her best to get the names right.

The week we visited a controversy was bubbling up around the mayor and the police chief he hired and now wants to fire. From what I could gather, the police chief arrested his cousin, the mayor, on a variety of driving charges after the mayor went to the aid of his daughter at a police roadblock set up to check for drunk drivers.

In many ways, Union Springs shares values we like to associate with the Island. People greet each other with the familiarity that comes from living and working in a closely knit community. "It's small, but we have a big heart," Donna Smith, a courthouse employee, told me.

But it is the politeness, rooted in the historic gentility of the South and exemplified time and again by our host, Charles, that strikes a first-time visitor. How you all doin'? How's your momma?

How's your daddy? First names receive a mister or a miss in front, if the person being addressed is older and familiar. For example, Coop would be known as Mr. Coop along the shores of one of the area's many well-stocked bass lakes.

These Southern protocols were observed on the street and in one of the more popular dining establishments in town, the one-room, cinder-block Hilltop Grill, a local racial melting pot. Entire families dressed in hunting camo sit side by side with lawyers, local office workers, and Alabama State Police officers. One can order a double bacon cheeseburger for $4.79, a chicken gizzards dinner with two sides for $5.59, and if for some reason you wanted to eat it, you would find okra listed as a side dish for $1.39.

Bullock County is a sportsman's playground. The deer season runs to the end of January. Turkey are plentiful, and wild pigs, a growing problem because of the destruction they cause to crops and woodlands, are hunted year-round. Many Islanders who do not hunt regard deer hunting as a means to eliminate a growing problem. In Bullock County and surrounding areas, hunting in all its forms is an essential part of the economy.

Signs welcome deer hunters from around the country. Farmers and landowners augment their incomes by leasing large tracts at about $10 an acre. And it is unusual to pass a field in which there is not a wooden box deer blind.

Plantations of thousands of acres are tilled, cut, and burned to provide ideal native grassland habitat for quail, a bird once native to the Vineyard. One of the better known is the Sedgefield Plantation, a property of approximately 14,000 acres that dates to the 1920s and was once the estate of the now deceased avid bird hunter L.B. Maytag, of appliance company fame.

"A lot of people in Alabama are outdoor people," Charles Klinck told me as we drove to have dinner in the steel storage building his friend Jim Smith and his wife, Sandra, had outfitted with a full kitchen for just such occasions.

The guests that night included a group of Waffle House executives, who leased Jim's property to deer hunt. "I met his daddy, Grady Smith, 18 years ago," said Joe Anchors from Atlanta, highlighting the longstanding bond.

Joe was surprised to learn that Coop and I had never heard of or been to a Waffle House. "You can't swing a cat without hittin' one," one of the Georgians said in disbelief.

The gathering began, as did several others we attended, with our host gathering us together for a prayer. Jim, a respected farmer and businessman, framed his Southern eloquence and political views in a prayer that thanked Jesus for the safe arrival of his Yankee friends from Massachusetts — a state that he prayed would elect Scott Brown that evening — and for the food and friendship we were about to share. "Amen" echoed in the room.

Charles had asked Jim to serve grits to his Northern guests. A battle soon warmed over the proper cooking technique, until we had dueling pots of grits. Jenks Parker, a man of considerable land, wealth, and standing in the community who has the classic look and bearing of Andrew Jackson, told me with some authority, "The fact is grits have to cook for a long, long time."

Most everyone stepped up to the stove with an opinion about the grits boiling in the water. To get near the stove they needed to step over a dog that lay on a mat smack in the way, but nobody seemed to mind.

"What's wrong with that dog?" one of the Georgians asked. "Old age, arthritis, and he's been run over," Jim said. "And he died twice."

"Poor Willy," Heather said.

Coop had brought a flat of oysters produced by Jack Blake of Sweet Neck Farm in Katama Bay. As Coop began to shuck, a big guy from Louisiana, the aforementioned coon ass, picked up a Katama oyster in his meaty hands and examined it. "Is that for real," Mr. Frank asked, as he examined the oyster's clean shell color and uniform shape. He joined Coop shucking. The Islander and the Cajun made quite a pair. He agreed that the Vineyard oysters were some of the prettiest and best tasting he had experienced. High praise from a Cajun, Jim said.

Later in the week, Coop and I each shot deer in one of Jim's fields. We hunted from separate, elevated plywood box blinds out-fitted with old office chairs that squeaked each time we shifted position. When he dropped us off, Jim told us what to say if we should find our blinds occupied. "Tell 'em that Jim said to get their asses outta there," he instructed.

(from left) Charles Klinck, Robert Morer, Willy "Bird" Owens and Cooper Gilkes at Shenandoah Plantation, Union Springs, Alabama.

"Got that?" I asked Coop. We brought the deer to one of the many processing operations. In our case, that meant driving to a farm and leaving our deer in a walk-in cooler with "24 hour drop off box" spray painted in red on the side. It was already stuffed with more than 30 deer.

One morning, Coop and I were invited to hunt quail over pointers on a 500-acre property, part of the more than 4,000-acre Shenandoah Plantation. It is a sporting version of Disneyland.

The landscape consisted of rolling hills, stands of wood, and grasses and swamp. Quail and deer abound. An elegant country lodge for guests overlooked one of three bass ponds. A pair of bald eagles soared overhead. I would trade its managed beauty for any 500 acres of "natural" tick-infested scrub oak on the Vineyard. Quail, or bobwhite, were once common on the Vineyard. Were someone to propose a large scale measure to remove the thick understory and transform a portion of the Vineyard's scrub oak terrain into more suitable habitat, there would certainly be daunting regulatory challenges.

For many residents and visitors, a day afield consists of riding horses over ground as the dogs range up ahead. When a dog locates a bird, it freezes in a point. The hunter dismounts and walks to the side of the dog. On command the dog is released to flush the bird, or birds, from the cover. Then it is up to the hunter.

The day Coop and I visited Shenandoah we decided it would be wiser to stick with a mode of transportation we understood, a customized Jeep outfitted with two seats and gun racks in the front and kennels in the back. Willy Owens, known by his nickname, "Bird," drove the jeep and kept track of the dogs for our dog handler Robert Moorer.

Once the dog went on point, Robert would motion for Coop and me to go to either side. Robert would call to Bird to release his Lab, "Gator." It was his job to flush the birds. The action was often fast. One, two, or 20 birds might suddenly erupt from the grass.

Heather and Charles maintain a stable of horses and kennel of dogs. But one dog is favored above all others. Billy, an English setter formally known as "Ch. Panovski Billy Boy," holds multiple local and national titles that include the 1999 National Amateur Shooting Dog Championship. Now retired, Billy lives in the house surrounded by his many awards. In his prime, he was a much sought-after stud.

But the life of the celebrity stud is not all it is cracked up to be. "Some of those female dogs were mean and had to be artificially inseminated," Heather said. "But now Billy loves to go to the vet."

Our introduction to Union Springs social life came with this caution: "The bar is smoky, the drinks are strong and the atmosphere is classic." Heather told us the Union Springs Country Club is not fancy. She said that the only requirement is that you cannot wear a cap in the dining room. Coop and I were not disappointed.

We were the guests that night of the grand dame of Union Springs, Mrs. Bootie Smitherman, known to all as Miss Bootie. Among the other guests who joined us at our table in the cocktail lounge was Miss Ginger [Austin], chairman of the Republican Party in Bullock County, a woman with strong opinions on a variety of subjects.

Our waitress, Joellen Gray Smith, had volunteered to fill in for an absent employee. It was only her second night waitressing. "This is about as far from my real profession as you can be," she said as she placed another drink on the table.

Miss Bootie asked about Joellen's "daddy."

"He had to go to Atlanta to pick up Margaret Copeland," Joellen explained. "She was coming in on the 3:30 flight, and he had to go get her."

After Joellen left the table, Heather asked quietly, "Is she alive or dead?"

"She's going to be *daid*," Miss Bootie said. She turned to me with an explanation. "Her daddy's the funeral director."

Joellen, who works with her daddy, returned to the table cheerily.

"This is so totally opposite of my regular job," she said with a smile. "I don't usually get to talk to people."

A Walk on the Beach and New Friends Met Along the Way

President Obama missed an opportunity for an authentic Martha's Vineyard experience when he picked up a golf club instead of a fishing rod.
(August 2016)

PRESIDENT BARACK OBAMA departed Martha's Vineyard Sunday evening. Over the course of his sixteen-day vacation he played golf on 10 days, mostly teaming up with elite current and former NBA players, and wealthy businessmen with seasonal connections to the Island.

It is unfortunate that Barack Obama chose to spend most of his vacation time engaging in a sport that does little to distinguish the Vineyard from any other rolling piece of meticulously maintained green grass with lovely views. Had he asked me I would have advised him to try casting a lure among the rocks along the north shore for bass, troll off Devil's Bridge for blues or just rake up a bushel of clams in Menemsha Pond. He did not ask, and the closest he got to an authentic Vineyard fishing experience was a dinner plate upon which lay an exquisitely prepared piece of striped bass.

I was prompted to ponder what the president was missing after my encounter with a 25-foot Coast Guard patrol boat off Menemsha Hills in Vineyard Sound. The crew included a Coast Guardsman wearing a combat helmet who was tethered to a 50-caliber machine gun mounted on the bow, and three heavily armed men in the cabin. The boat came racing up to me at full speed, wake spray flying as though they were auditioning for a recruiting film.

My 18-foot Tashmoo skiff was armed with one fly rod and two spinning rods. I was about one-quarter of a mile from the beach heading for Menemsha Harbor, passing well offshore — I thought — from the Obama vacation house set back from the sand cliffs of Menemsha Hills.

The stern but polite person in the wheelhouse informed me that there was a "1,000-yard federal security zone" in place (that's more than half a mile) and I would have to go offshore another 100 yards or so. Really, I thought to myself, is this necessary — the president is golfing and dining out in a lot closer proximity to the general public, and here we are on Vineyard Sound where there is a clear view of everything on the water, but I have to make an even bigger loop — hey, who am I to argue with a machine gun?

So I proceeded north and thought about the notion of the imperial presidency and the layers of insulation that now accompany the job. And I came to the conclusion that our presidents ought to go fishing, if for no other reason than it is a good way to meet ordinary people — maybe not those that contribute $25,000 campaign checks — but good people nonetheless.

I was reminded of the equalizing effect of fishing when I came across some photos I took in late February, when Norma and I visited our friends Ed and Laurel at their vacation home on Barbados. On previous visits I would walk along the beautiful beach and often encounter local fishermen. Bajans are quite friendly, and it was always easy to talk fishing.

The shore fishing is not particularly good around this volcanic-spawned island, but mahi-mahi, tuna, and barracuda are just offshore. I brought a light spinning rod to cast from the shore, and packed extra lures I thought would be of some use offshore, not to use but to give away.

Colvin was bottom-fishing near a rocky point for anything he could catch to eat. His tackle consisted of two broken spinning reels, one of which he jammed with a piece of wood to keep it from revolving freely, and heavy surf rods with broken guides. For weight he used lead pulled from an old car battery. We chatted about fishing, and I told him I would bring him luck. I was quite happy when my prediction came true and he caught a pretty reef fish, a chub of some type, no bigger than an average scup.

Colvin holds up a small reef fish he caught.

Colvin said he had been an amateur boxer. He said he used to fish from a boat but something, which he declined to elaborate on with a hint of darkness, had happened.

I handed him several lures, including some Deadly Dicks, and a Martha's Vineyard Bass and Bluefish Derby fishing cap. I told him about our Island's annual fishing tournament — the center-piece of so many Island friendships. Colvin was genuinely happy about his new hat and his new friend, as was I.

Fisherman Wilton Broome.

A few days later I hiked up the beach to one of the government-run fish markets adjacent to John Moore's rum bar, an island landmark where those of high and low station drink glasses of white rum. Fishing boats were pulled up on the beach in various states of repair.

Fisherman Wilton Broome, along with Patrick Thomas, and Shaun Roach were limin' (hanging around) by Wilton's fishing boat. I might have been on the dock in Menemsha. We talked about the fishing — been kind of slow — and the lack of bait. I reached into my pack and pulled out a handful of tuna lures Cooper Gilkes had generously given me to take down to the island (I'd asked for anything old he didn't need, but Coop being Coop, he handed me several new lures). The guys thought the lures were great, and I had three new friends.

On my way back I watched a woman swim out from the beach holding a spinning rod in her hand. Treading water, she started casting. I was impressed with her enthusiasm and took several photos.

When she returned to shore we chatted. She was a bit leery of my photo taking, but I assured Rochelle, "You're a very intrepid fisherman, and Island fishermen on Martha's Vineyard appreciate that quality." Rochelle (her friends call her Rocky) was from the Caribbean, but lives in Montreal, Canada.

On Martha's Vineyard there are a Colvin, a Wilton, and a Rocky — I would not want to name names, but I do think that Barack Obama would enjoy meeting them. Were he to return for the 71st Derby, which begins Sunday, Sept. 11, and ends Oct. 15, he would see an Island not measured by 18 holes in the ground.

Before we left Barbados, I decided I would leave my spinning rod and reel with Colvin. I looked for him on the beach and amid the small houses on a hillside where he said he lived, but did not find him.

About one week after we returned to the Vineyard I received an email from Laurel. She said that returning from a stroll past the rocky point that morning, she chanced upon a man "sitting on the cement walk holding a fishing line leading straight into the sea. I asked him what kept the line taut, and he said, lead. I asked whether he was the one that our friend had told us about, who made his weights out of battery parts. He got all bright at that, and said, 'Nelson.'"

And when I received that email I smiled and said, "Colvin."

Islanders

"… I once found a list of diseases as yet unclassified
by medical science, and among these there occurred
the word Islomania, which was described as a rare
but by no means unknown affliction of spirit. There
are people … who find islands somehow irresistible.
The mere knowledge that they are on an island, a
little world surrounded by the sea, fills them with an
indescribable intoxication. These born "Islomanes"…
are direct descendants of the Atlanteans"

LAWRENCE DURRELL, REFLECTIONS ON A MARINE VENUS

Roberto Germani Catches a
Bonito by the Skin of His Teeth

The best fishing is all a matter of proportion
(August 1991)

THERE ARE FISHERMEN who chase thousand-pound marlin in forty-eight-foot sport fisherman strapped into $2,000 fighting chairs with a crew of three. Roberto Germani chases seven-pound bonito in an eight-foot canoe with a lightweight fly rod by himself.

He was fly fishing off the Oak Bluffs Steamship Authority ferry dock in his familiar green canoe. The wind and the current had the bait and bonito all swirling on the up-current side.

Suddenly, a bonito hit his fly, and Roberto thought to himself, "Oh geez, I've got a problem," because instead of heading out, the fish was headed into the dock. He tightened up on the drag as much as he dared while the fish took his line around the end piling of the slip.

He did have problems. He had to keep his rod tip up so the line would be on the greased part of the piling instead of rubbing against the barnacles, but he also had to get his anchor up and chase the fish. So he stuck the fly rod into his mouth, keeping it as high as he could, then pulled up the anchor and began back-paddling as fast as he could go, while listening to his line go "zzzzzzzz" around the piling as the fish swam into the first ferry slip.

— 229 —

"Roberto Germani fishing the Gut,"
oil painting by Kib Bramhall.

Meanwhile, he says, "the fly reel handle is whackin' around, goin' 'bidda, bidda, bidda' in my beard."

Roberto managed to turn the corner minus a few whiskers and realized that the fish was going straight into the slip. So he put the paddle down, took the fly rod out of his mouth, and started reeling in, but while doing that, the wind and tide prepared to take him through the other side of the dock.

Into his mouth went the fly rod and he started back paddling his way out of the slip leading the fish, but all the time Roberto was figuring there's no way he will get this fish. Not on a barbless little no. 8 hook. But he managed to keep tension on the fish and back it out of the slip.

"Great," he thought. Now he had the canoe and the fish out. Down goes the paddle, out of the mouth comes the fly rod.

He figured, at last, after 15 minutes he was free and clear, then the fish headed right for a guy's anchor line. Roberto yelled, "Pull your anchor," but there was no response. He yelled again — no response. Roberto says, "I might just as well've been yellin' 'Go shopping at

K-mart,' I mean he didn't have a clue and now I see the fish go around his anchor line and I can feel the friction of the fly line on it."

Back in his teeth went the fly rod as he paddled after the fish. He yelled again, "Pull up your anchor." The other guy answered, "What?"

He finally figured out what's going on and managed to pull up the anchor and get the line off.

Roberto could not believe it. The fish was still on and taking out line and he was free of everybody. He thinks he might start to settle down and try to get the fish in. The fly rod comes out of his mouth, he drops his anchor and starts reeling in line, thinking "what a fish" and wondering when the backing is going to part, or the hook's going to open, or the tippet is going to break.

He's wondering all these things thinking he's all alone when all of a sudden — BUMP! A fisherman in a small tin boat with another bonito has crashed into his canoe.

Now that fish wraps itself around his anchor line as the small boat bangs against his canoe and Roberto's fish is headed to the jetty. Back into his mouth goes the fly rod as he takes the other fisherman's small spinning rod and passes it around his anchor line until he is free.

Roberto warily tries to settle down. He starts reeling in and once he's able to stop shaking he stands up and can see the fish. Around and around the canoe the bonito swims.

"I can't figure, the fish shoulda been dead ten minutes ago, right, long dead, and the hook shoulda opened, and the tippet shoulda broken, and here I am still with this fish. Well, I finally get 'im into the canoe and he's as dead as Lazarus. You know, his gills are wide open, his mouth is wide open and he's got all these lines. I'm lookin' at him and I think, I gotta bring this fish to life. So I'm swishing him back and forth and I started thinking, desperate situations call for desperate measures: CPR!

"So I cup my hands around his gill plates and I start pumping his gill plates like I'm clapping my hands and I'm pumpin' and pumpin' and pumpin'.

"And I'm thinking I must be crazy but I keep doing this for a while and all of a sudden, I see a change in color. Well, I'll be a son-of-a-bitch it's working, so I keep it up and keep it up and after a while I see his jaw start moving and I feel a shudder. So I keep going and going, then I put my hand under his caudal fin and now his gills are moving by themselves. Finally, I give him a little push and he slowly swims away."

No white whale, no marlin on a hand-line but still an epic battle with a truly fine ending. The best fishing is really all a matter of proportion.

Roberto Germani died January 19, 1992 at his home on Martha's Vineyard at the age of 58.

Jimmy "Yank 'n Crank" Goes Toe-to-Fin

No fancy tackle needed; just a stout rod, heavy line and a willingness to wake up early in the morning.
(August 1994)

BEFORE SUNRISE, WHEN the eastern horizon holds only the faintest promise of morning, is the best time to head to big bridge. Few vehicles interrupt the early hour quiet of Beach Road and the bridge railing takes on the atmosphere of a neighborhood street corner as the regulars set up their bait rods with coffee in hand. And no fisherman is more regular than Jimmy Klingensmith of Edgartown.

"I don't even set the alarm anymore — four a.m — it's automatic," Jimmy said.

Jimmy Klingensmith has taken more than his share of big fish from big bridge, which spans the channel that connects Sengekontacket Pond and Nantucket Sound on the Oak Bluffs-Edgartown town line. During the derby,

Jimmy "Yank and Crank" on big bridge.

when everyone else is trying to figure out where the leaders caught their fish, there is never any question when Jimmy has a fish on the board about where he caught it. Big bridge is his spot and he keeps a close watch on every swirl in the moving current with the practiced eye of someone who knows his neighborhood.

The largest striper he ever caught at the bridge was a 47-pounder, and a few years ago he caught a 15.74-pound blue during the derby that was a contender. "Held on good to the last day," he said with the chagrin of a fisherman. But Jimmy doesn't rest on the fish caught yesterday. He said he arrives at the bridge every morning with the idea that there's a big one out there.

And Jimmy knows how to tackle the big ones without breaking off his line on the bridge pilings where the big stripers hold, which accounts for his nickname: Jimmy "yank and crank."

Jimmy rigs up a stout eleven-foot rod suitable for pole vaulting with a length of eighty pound test monofilament line to which he adds a six-foot steel leader. This is toe-to-fin, trading punches fishing. When he does hook up the resulting splashing and thrashing sounds under the bridge are akin to a barroom brawl. Jimmy just leans back, lets the rod bend over on the railing and makes sure the fish can't even think about going under the bridge and wrapping around the railings.

But one night he really slugged it out. He'd gone to the bridge with his heavy rod and the knowledge that some big bass were hanging underneath in the shadows. Only he didn't have a reel. Instead, he'd just run the heavy mono through the rod guides and tied it off around the butt of the rod — a cane pole on steroids.

"I was fishin' that meat pole — no reel — and hooked into a nice bass that really tore that water up," he said. "You know, I only had about eight feet of line and this guy who was fishin' on the jetty, he comes runnin' up to me to see what all the commotion was about and when he saw my rod he goes, 'My God, he stripped your reel and all.'

"And I let him think it. I didn't even comment. I just let it go."

Irene Henley Still Casts Straight

The 82-year-old revisited Wasque Point and the pleasures of surfcasting.
(July 1995)

IRENE HENLEY OF Edgartown is 82 years old. She may not get as much distance as she did many years ago out of the custom 10-foot surf rod she built herself, but her form is still graceful. On Monday evening, she cast a white popping plug straight and true into the flowing current of Wasque rip and a sea of surfcasting memories.

The surf rods Irene built herself still hang from ceiling hooks in her house. An assortment of jigs and plugs sit in white buckets placed neatly on shelves in a small entrance way. A set of waders hangs in the garage. And while diabetes may have affected her eyesight, Irene still appears trim enough to respond to news of any fish blitz along the beach even if she doesn't get out of the house much.

Mary Jo Goodrich works for the Visiting Nurse Association. Last fall and winter she was assigned to see Irene who hadn't been well. Mary Jo was fascinated by the fishing rods, tackle, and pictures that Irene had in the house. But more intriguing were the stories told by Irene of fishing on the Vineyard — of Islanders and big stripers, of beach buggies and blitzes.

Mary Jo Goodrich and mentor Irene
Henley at Wasque.

Irene told Mary Jo, "If you live on this Island you have to fish."
And Irene told Mary Jo she would teach her.

The rods were brought down from the hooks. The tackle, so
neatly put away, was gathered, and the two women went down to
the beach where Irene began to teach Mary Jo the finer points of
casting. Mary Jo said, "Irene is the one who taught me, it's not a
fishing pole, it is a fishing rod."

Irene moved to the Island with her family when she was five
years old. Her father owned a farm in Edgartown and, other than
a short off-Island stint, she has lived here all her life. She says she
took up surfcasting because she had asthma and found the exercise and salt air beneficial.

As can any good fisherman, Irene can still recount her fishing
exploits in great detail. There was the day she caught three stripers and one blue — an 18-pounder from Wasque. But Irene would
be the first to mention that, fish or no fish, the best part was just

being out there. Wasque on the southeast corner of Chappy was and remains one of her favorite fishing spots.

Monday evening I took Irene and Mary Jo out for a ride to Chappy. It had been many years since Irene had been on the Chappy ferry. In her day, a breach in Katama and not plovers was the only reason to divert beach buggies. Terns hovered in a knot in Edgartown harbor. "Probably bonito," Irene said, demonstrating the instincts of a fisherman.

At Wasque, Irene carefully selected plugs for her and Mary from a small lure bag worn over her shoulder. She made a cast and brought the plug dancing back over the sea. A smile crossed her face. Her pupil, Mary Jo, also made a fine cast as Irene looked on approvingly.

Does Mary Jo have the "right stuff?" I asked.

"Absolutely," answered Irene.

Mention Irene Henley to any Island fisherman from the days when 10 people at Wasque were a crowd and Islanders could fish pretty much where they wanted. They will speak admiringly about a woman who could hold her own where the surf met the sand.

"Those are good memories," Fred Hehre, now a lawyer in Vineyard Haven, said. He was just a kid and didn't have a car but would walk down the beach to go fishing. Irene would give the young fisherman a ride home and swap fishing stories along the way.

Irene remembered "Freddy" Hehre with a chuckle. "I would smile. You know, he would come up and say, 'Irene, can I fish beside you? I'd say 'Sure, there's plenty of room, Freddy.'"

Cooper Gilkes laughed at the mention of Irene as he recalled sitting at the opening when the ocean had breached Norton Point beach. He and his friends had a stack of bass and were a mile from their car parked at Katama.

"And who should be coming down the beach but Irene. She helped us load those bass into her old square-back jeep and got us back to the road. We had to take the back seat out of our old Dodge just to get the fish in," and he added with a laugh, recounting the experience, "we lost the muffler on the way to the market."

"Irene was just incredible," Coop said, "one of the only ladies at the time fishing." And in praise he added, "She'd fish right there at Wasque, right with the guys bringing fish in."

I ran into Fred Hehre at the coffee shop across the street and told him I took Irene fishing. I added, "She still casts straight."

"What more could you ask for?" Fred said with a smile, and we both nodded in agreement, thinking of Irene Henley.

Irene Henley died peacefully on Friday, June 15, 2001.

Fisherman Albert "Angie" Angelone, Presidential Protector

The spirit of friendships made on the beach endure.
(August 2006)

I FIRST MET ALBERT Peter Angelone in Coop's. I knew him as Angie, a kind of quirky, friendly guy who loved to fish often alone and at odd hours of the day. He was a hard fisherman on an Island of hard fisherman distinguished by the fact that he was always ready to provide a helpful hint about where the fish might be hitting.

When I would find his car parked at a location where I intended to fish I considered it to be as good a sign of fish as terns diving on bait. But I did not have his staying power. His car would often be there when I arrived and be there when I left.

Angie spoke in clipped phrases and laced his conversation with hard to figure references. He was always asking me, "You know what I mean?" But more often than not, I didn't know what he meant.

Unfailingly polite and courteous, he called me Mr. Sigelman. "Angie, call me Nelson," I told him after we first met. "Okay, okay, Mr. Sigelman," he said.

Angie was not one of those guys who talked about what he did before he arrived on the Vineyard. There was no bragging, no war stories, just an occasional cryptic mention that provided a hint of some type of police work, but not much more.

Secret Service agent Albert P. Angelone, standing in front of President
Gerald Ford's limousine, reacts to a gunshot on Sept. 22, 1975.

He was also not the sort to brag about fish caught (and he
caught plenty of fish) or anything else. The closest he ever came
to that was when we started talking about deer hunting with black
powder rifles and he dug out an aged photo from his car of a big
buck he had shot with a flintlock rifle.

Angie said he no longer hunted. When I asked him why he just
shrugged off the question. He never mentioned the wear and tear on
his body that made hiking in the woods and dragging out a deer problematic — or the fingers he lost when an Israeli agent being trained
in the U.S. slammed the door of an armored limousine on his hand.

Funny what we do not know about the people we meet. I wish
now I'd spent more time talking to Angie.

Saturday he died. I had the opportunity to get to know Angie
much better over the past few days writing his obituary.

I never ever would have imagined that the funny guy with the New York accent had once been one of the Secret Service's top undercover agents. But well before he retired to the safety and security we take for granted on Martha's Vineyard, Angie was fighting crime in the front-line trenches.

He worked undercover in some of the country's toughest neighborhoods investigating and arresting counterfeiters. And he earned a reputation among his peers as a man who could always be counted on in a tight fix.

On Monday I talked to George Rogers, the Secret Service's assistant director of the office of inspection. The fact that he took the time to speak to me was an obvious testament to Angie's status.

When George was younger, the two men worked the streets of New York together. There were too many stories to tell and those that he could tell me I would not be able to write about.

George said he was from upstate New York, a country kid who liked to hunt and fish. When Angie learned that George liked to fish he assured him that despite the fact that they were in the heart of New York City they could still catch fish.

Angie told George to meet him at 5 am near their office located near where the World Trade Center used to be. They drove out to Kennedy Airport and parked.

"We walked out past the big tall weeds, willows, junk refrigerators and broken down rusty cars and ended up fishing right off the approach of some runway," recalled George. "And I don't know what it was, it must have been about every six minutes, one of these jets came over, but you know what? We caught fish."

Over the roar of the planes Angie said to George, "I told you I'd show you where there were fish."

Later, Angie was transferred from undercover to the presidential protection division. George said that some people questioned the wisdom of moving the street-wise undercover agent to the more visible post. In the end Angie turned out to be terrific, he said.

The most public demonstration of his steadfastness came while he was guarding President Gerald Ford during a visit to San Francisco. The president was by his limousine when a shot rang out.

A photograph taken that day shows people ducking behind the limousine. Angie is shown standing alone, on the other side of the limo, his hand reaching for his gun and his eyes scanning for the source of the danger.

It was an incident that as far as I can tell none of his Vineyard friends knew anything about. Even after he discovered the joy and peace of fishing on the Vineyard, Angie still shied away from publicity. On the rare occasions he let me reference a catch, he would always remind me, "no pictures." I just put it down to him being a quirky guy.

Angie was one of those guys who did not need company to go fishing. The fish kept him company. Dogfish Bar, Bend in the Road Beach, Mink Meadows or Chappy, Angie was apt to show up anywhere. Because he fished almost every day he was also apt to turn up where the fish were and the fishermen weren't.

I often came across Angie fishing alone up at Dogfish, his pipe an unmistakable marker even in the dark. He always had a good word. "How ya doin'?" he'd ask me.

In recent years, I ran into Angie fishing with his wife Mary Ann. As any fisherman will attest, a husband and wife that can live together and fish together require true love and devotion to stay together.

"When we first got married the one thing he said to me is I've got to have a week to be able to hunt in New York," said Mary Ann from the small home they built in West Tisbury. "And by the time we moved to Maryland a week had become, God, I don't know how many weeks."

Later, after he was injured, he could no longer hunt. "But he always fished," said Mary Ann, "no matter where we lived he always fished."

Angie fished a lot. But Mary Ann said that Angie always told her he wasn't a real fisherman.

"I think he thought a real fisherman spends 23 hours out fishing," she said with a laugh. "But he was a good fisherman and the past couple of years I started to fish with him. And I've got to say he was the most selfless person. He would tie my lures, he would take the fish off the hook — otherwise the fish would have died by the time I got it off — but he didn't want me to get hurt and I think he was happier when I caught a big fish then when he did."

Angie was a part of a Vineyard fraternity bound by a love of fishing. He left the house early to go fishing Saturday morning. When he did not show up for an appointment later that morning Mary Ann contacted friends and fishermen and asked them to help locate her husband.

By late afternoon fishermen were looking around the Island's beaches for some sign of his vehicle. Early that evening, acting on a hunch about where Angie might have gone, Cooper Gilkes and Robert Morrison, went to a spot near Mink Meadows and found Angie.

There is no sadness in the fact that he died on an Island he loved doing what he loved, but he will be missed.

Mary Ann told me, "Island fishermen are the greatest people in the world." Angie was definitely one of them

Herbert Hancock: Island Gunners Blended Purpose and Craft

Smart, wary and tough to fool describes this hunter as well as the black duck.
(January 1999)

BEFORE TRANSPLANTED CITY folk defined Vineyard rural quality, when a black dog was considered a hunting companion and not a souvenir icon, Island waterfowlers shot over decoys carved by men able to imbue blocks of cedar with natural honesty and grace.

These days, molded plastic has replaced wood as the material of choice, and spacious houses stand in place of unadorned cabins along the shores of the Vineyard's great ponds. But a duck hunter can still find a spot for a well-placed blind to sit with a dog, and one Islander still carves wooden decoys that conjure up stories of mornings spent duck hunting on the Vineyard's windswept coastal marshes.

Herbert R. Hancock, lobsterman and long-time Chilmark selectman, began duck hunting with his father and grandfather in the marshes and ponds of Chilmark. It was his job to pick up the ducks the men had shot.

"I was just a kid; I was doing it for fun, but my father was doing it for something to eat," says Herbert about his first trip.

Herbert Hancock shapes a decoy head.

"To me just sitting out there, with maybe 20 decoys in front of us there, and the bluebills were flying from the east out of the sunrise and comin' into the decoys, I'll tell you, that was something for a kid. I'd never seen anything like that before."

Herbert started carving decoys more than 50 years ago for the same reason that his great-grandfather — Russell Hancock, a whaler, fisherman, and farmer — carved them: to attract ducks. It was a time when Islanders went hunting and fishing to put food on the table and could little afford to buy decoys.

"I wanted some bluebill and widgeon to go duck hunting," says Herbert. He decided he could make a better decoy than the few he had available.

"I liked to do carpentry work in the summer and was around a wood shop with tools, and extra pieces of wood lying around there, so I just carved duck decoys," he says with no reference to his own skills and natural ability.

In high school he sat in study hall and carved decoy heads. The graduating class was all of 27 students. Later, when he went away to Wentworth Institute in Boston, he sold his decoys for $3 apiece.

"I thought I was doing real good," he says.

David Flanders of Chilmark went to high school with Herbert, and the two were frequent hunting companions over the years.

"We got a lot of birds and had a lot of fun," he says about mornings spent hunting over a collection of decoys set out before sunrise on Squibnocket Pond.

Including one morning when a city newspaper photographer accompanied the two Islanders to take some photographs. A flight of geese came in and Herbert shot one.

"It came out of the air and landed right on top of the guy taking pictures, came right down and whacked 'im," says David with a laugh that cuts across years.

"It was a great life to go and to be there when the sun came up and the birds were comin' and everything was happening. Part of it was just being out there, it was very beautiful."

Herbert stopped duck hunting almost 15 years ago when ducks, and opportunities to go places he had hunted as a boy, slowly disappeared. But his love and appreciation of wooden decoys, particularly the decoys of Vineyard carvers, never diminished.

Most days, if the weather is good Herbert tends his lobster pots. But when winter winds blow and he cannot work outside, he still likes to sit at his workbench with a block of wood and a draw knife carving decoys. If he and his wife Billie go on vacation, wood blocks still to be carved into decoy heads are packed in his bag.

"They're more decorative now," Herbert admits, "a little fancier than you need for duck hunting."

But they are finished and painted with the memory of a water-fowler. They are often given away as gifts.

Asked what is his favorite duck to carve, Herbert says, "The black duck. I just like the black duck."

The black duck is, one expert Island waterfowler says, the quintessential indigenous Island duck. It is smart, wary, and tough to fool — qualities Herbert has projected as selectman for more than 35 years in a changing Chilmark. Spare and economical in word and deed, he gives no long-winded statements. Asked what makes a good decoy, he cocks his head and with an expression that he reserves for the obvious, he answers direct and to the point: "If it looks like a duck."

Old decoys by recognized carvers have taken on a value that the hunters who shot over them could never have imagined. Modern decoys that have never spent a day in the icy water, carved by talented craftsmen who have never watched a duck flare, command a high price.

Despite a collection which includes works by many Island carvers, Herbert has no decoys made by his great-grandfather. All were stolen or sold before he began his collection. Asked what is his favorite decoy, Herbert points out a black duck made by Benjamin D. Smith of Oak Bluffs, born in 1866. Plain and unadorned, it carries a simple natural grace in every subtle curve.

"He made it just for duck hunting," Herbert says. "It is just a damn good lookin' duck, there's no prettier one really."

Noted Island artist, muralist, and decoy collector Stan Murphy, in his book "Martha's Vineyard Decoys" (David R. Godine, Publisher, 1978), describes Ben Smith as a carver of some of the finest decoy ducks ever seen, a loner "who made his decoys for the ducks only, not for men, yet his carvings are a distillation of great natural talent, the keenest powers of observation, and superb technique."

In the conclusion of his book he says of the old decoys: "They were made only to toll the birds, not to leave for posterity the evidence of man's ability to create from common materials things of truth and occasional great beauty. The secret of the fascination of old decoys, of the endless variations of their small forms, lies somehow in the word unselfconscious. They pay no conscious homage, as do other art forms, to God or to man or to ego; their sole intent is to convince a living duck that they too are alive. Thus their rare integrity and finally, their immortality."

Mr. Murphy, sitting in his comfortable living room discussing wood decoys and mornings spent watching the sun rise over a spread of decoys years ago, says, "There were no artistic pretensions among the Island carvers of a generation ago. Their work was absolutely honest."

Herbert R. Hancock, a builder, lobsterman, and decoy carver, who as selectman for 37 consecutive years guided the small town of Chilmark on the Island of Martha's Vineyard with Yankee common sense in decision making and thrift in speech and spending, died April 26, 2001 at his home on Middle Road after a short battle with cancer. He was 71.

Olga Was a Derby Fisherman in Heart and Soul

Olga Hirshhorn counted presidents, artists, and movers and shakers among her friends, but I think she preferred hanging out with fishermen.
(October 2015)

OLGA HIRSHHORN DID not fish as many days, or catch as many big fish, as many Derby fishermen, but she had as much heart and soul and spirit as anyone who ever walked into the weigh station and dropped a big striper on the scale.

Olga died Saturday at the age of 95 in her winter home in Florida. When I received a copy of her obituary from her son, John Cunningham, I said I wanted to use a photo of Olga in the weigh station. "Mother would love it," John emailed back.

My introduction was anything but ordinary. It was 1995. Olga Hirshhorn — doyenne of the art world, wife of the founder of the Hirshhorn Museum in Washington, D.C., art collector, grandmother, and irrepressible world traveler — had bid on a fishing trip with Cooper Gilkes, Island fisherman and tackle shop owner, and me, the scribe for the adventure as part of the Possible Dreams fundraiser auction.

When I learned who had bid, I told Coop we were taking out a grandmother who was big in the art world. I told Coop we would probably be out a few hours and she would want to come in. Boy, was I mistaken.

Olga Hirshhorn sports a derby cap as she brings a fish to the weigh station.

So what did a woman who had lived on a palatial estate, sat next to presidents, ridden on elephants in India, and collected art around the world have in common with an Edgartown tackle shop owner and a fishing columnist? Simple. She loved to fish.

I wrote about our first trip, one of many that would follow — raising thousands of dollars for Martha's Vineyard Community Services in the process — in a fishing column titled, "Ms. Hirshhorn Reels in the Possible Bass."

"It was past noon, and we had been trying to hook up since 7 am. Coop put the throttle down on his 18-foot Boston Whaler Montauk and we began to bump across the water as we left Edgartown Harbor heading for Vineyard Sound. It had been dead calm when we made the decision to give up chasing albies and bonito and look for some bass, but the wind had started to pick up, raising a light chop.

"I was standing next to Cooper and holding on to the center console rail. Olga sat behind us with her back turned to the breeze. She was wearing a white Derby cap, a blue windbreaker, and had slipped her feet, slippers and all, into my size 10 beat-up blue sneakers to keep her feet warm, giving her feet a decidedly Ringling Brothers appearance. It was a fashion look perfectly in keeping with the Derby, if not the lady.

"'Olga,' I shouted above the noise of the outboard and salt spray, 'we may not have impressed you yet but you sure have impressed us.'

'You've got that right,' Cooper added.

"... The popular fundraiser for Community Services had offered a variety of 'possible dreams,' including walk-on parts on popular shows such as "Seinfeld' and 'Chicago Hope,' and lunch with publisher Katharine Graham, dreams that reflected the Island's ties to off-Island influence and celebrity. But Olga wasn't looking for that. She was interested in an Island experience.

"We arranged to meet Olga and her guest, Nina Davis, at 7 am at the Edgartown dock, hoping the weather would allow us to fish in the harbor or Cape Poge for bonito or false albacore. After seining up some fresh sand eels, we started our way up what had become 'false albacore alley,' the route followed by a small flotilla of derby fishermen as they pursued the hard-charging albies.

"Small pods of albies were erupting in Edgartown Harbor as boats danced around each other, rods at the ready; at the gut, fishermen lined the bank. But the action was slow and scattered, so we headed for East Beach.

"The day had cleared up, the wind had dropped, and the sea was a light emerald green. Nina lay down on the deck and enjoyed the sun, happy to relax from the task of remodeling her new house. Olga held her rod, following Coop's instructions on how to play the bait. She wasn't interested in reeling in a fish that someone else hooked; Olga was there to fish.

"By noon the only hit had come from a Spanish mackerel that severed the line with the neatness of a razor. Coop and I discussed strategy, determined to find fish. 'How do you feel about trying for some bass?' I asked Olga and Nina. 'We're thinking of going back in so Coop can grab some eels and heavier rods at his shop. Are you up for heading out again?'

Olga's reply reflected the philosophical yet practical approach needed by every good Derby fisherman. 'I don't have to be anywhere until 10 am tomorrow,' she answered. Coop and I decided we really liked Olga.

"We headed off for the sound without Nina. She had enjoyed fishing and loved sunning, but in general felt the need to chase down the people who were supposed to be working on her house. I suggested that during Derby time she had a better chance of finding them with us.

"Vineyard Sound was flat calm as we pulled up off Cedar Tree Neck. Coop rigged up two heavy rods with squirming eels and dropped them to the bottom, handing one rod to Olga. I dropped some sand eels over, looking for a fluke. Almost immediately I had a hit, and I traded rods with Olga. She reeled up a nice sea bass. Another quickly followed, and another. The lady was hot.

"Suddenly the rod doubled over. 'I've got one,' Olga shouted. It was no sea bass from the look of the rod, and Coop coached as Olga tried to fight the fish to the surface. The line snapped.

"'Oh, dammit! Can I swear?' Olga said, flushed with a fisherman's combination of excitement and disappointment.

"Coop just nodded and consoled, 'You go right ahead.'

"It was getting late in the afternoon, and we started to head back around West Chop, when bonito and false albacore started bursting from the water. Coop anchored up and, before long, Olga was fighting a fish to the surface. Into the net came a bluefish.

"'Oh golly, that was fun,' declared Olga with a wide smile. A nice 32-inch striper would follow. But the albies and bonito bursting periodically around us proved more elusive. Still, it was exciting.

"Around 6:30 pm, we pulled up to Owen Park dock in Vineyard Haven so Olga could walk to her home on Franklin Street instead of riding back to Edgartown in the boat. It was more than 11 hours after we'd started, and Olga had gone the distance. Coop quickly cleaned one of the sea bass, but we didn't have a bag. No matter. Mrs. Olga Hirshhorn took the sea bass strung on a piece of fishing line and went walking up the road."

Years later, I still remember her walking up the road with that fish on a stringer. Coop and I were exhausted. Olga was off to a movie date.

There are people who like to fish, and there are fishermen. The difference is the gulf that separates affection and passion.

And one of the wonderful things about fishermen is that no matter what they do or where they come from, there is something that connects them with other fishermen. I was thinking about that connection after I heard that Olga died, and how lucky I was to fish with her.

The Works of Stan Murphy: A Singular Island Retrospective

It had been 50 years since the artist had attended a show of his works.
(August 2002)

O N A WARM August Sunday afternoon with the scent of a dry, freshly cut Vineyard meadow hanging in the air, West Tisbury painter Stan Murphy did what he has done only once before during an artistic career spanning more than half a century. He attended a gallery opening of his own work.

The significance of his presence Sunday was a topic of conversation among the many friends, family, and admirers gathered under a white canopy set up in front of his small, weathered gallery on South Road. Mr. Murphy prefers to let his work speak for itself.

The show, which opened Sunday and continues through Friday, Sept. 6, is a selected retrospective of Island portraits which Mr. Murphy painted over the last 50 years, lent by their owners — including the Wampanoag Tribe, the town of West Tisbury, Island residents, and members of the Murphy family. None of the paintings are for sale, a fact which figured large in Mr. Murphy's willingness to attend the reception organized by his wife, Polly, and family members.

Artist Stan Murphy with self-portrait.

At its heart, the opening was really a gathering of friends and familiar faces, those standing conversing in the yard and those captured on canvas by Mr. Murphy over many years.

In an atmosphere reminiscent of a community potluck dinner, Mr. Murphy, 80, stood tall and lean, greeting neighbors and friends. Some, like Danny Bryant of Chilmark, pictured duck hunting with his dog Duchess in a Vineyard saltmarsh, also occupied a place on a gallery wall.

One woman said that walking into the gallery and seeing the images "was like walking into a roomful of friends, good people."

"Hi Claire," said Norma Sigelman after spotting a formal portrait of Claire Duys of Music Street, painted in 1981 when the violinist was 90. Reminiscing about the elegant equestrian, she added, "What a lady!"

Many of the paintings selected for the show reflect consistent themes in Mr. Murphy's life and art: respect for the outdoors, an appreciation of hard-working Islanders, and a strong sense of what binds the rural community of Martha's Vineyard. Above all it is his ability to understand and capture the essential spirit and character of his Island subjects that imbues Mr. Murphy's paintings with an authenticity that sets his work apart and has earned him recognition as the dean of Island painters.

A painting of Alfred Vanderhoop done in 1996 shows the respected Wampanoag tribal elder and lifelong fisherman in the stern of the Red Wing, the boat he used to fish local Island waters until his death. He wears the slightly doleful expression of a fisherman who has to work hard for a full haul.

In another painting, Milton Jeffers, "legendary on Chappaquiddick and Edgartown as a man who could do anything," according to a gallery note, stands at his forge holding a hammer in his powerful right arm.

The political life of a small Island town is reflected in Mr. Murphy's classic 1977 painting of the three West Tisbury selectmen, Alan Look, Everett Whiting, and John Alley, standing on the steps of the old town hall, now the West Tisbury police station. In another, titled "Officers of the West Tisbury Fire Department," painted in 1957, five firefighters strike relaxed and individual poses.

There are paintings of Mr. Murphy's friends. One portrait shows Tess Bramhall of West Tisbury, identified as a conservationist, sportswoman, and member of his golf foursome for over 20 years. There are portraits of friend and neighbor Virginia Mazer, outdoorsman and writer Nelson Bryant, and fellow West Tisbury painter Allen Whiting.

There are personally revealing portraits as well. One joyful painting done in 1955 shows his two daughters, Laura and Kitty, arms exuberantly outstretched, walking through a meadow of tall grass. According to the gallery note, the painting was done after both girls contracted rocky mountain spotted fever and it was clear they would survive. A self-portrait captures the artist's reserve. A slightly wry expression crosses his face, giving a hint of someone who is not as serious as he might appear.

As people milled throughout the gallery, one owner of three of Mr. Murphy's paintings said that while the artist has "always been a master of light," the change in his brush strokes was evident as one viewed the span of his work on display. "They just get richer and richer," he said.

Asked to describe the artist and the man, Tess Bramhall said, "The first word that comes to mind is that he is a perfectionist. He has extremely high standards for himself and for his art." She added, "He has a wonderful sense of humor and that shows in his work."

Nelson Bryant, longtime New York Times outdoor columnist and West Tisbury resident, said, "One thing you find out when you sit for him, he is a meticulous craftsman. You spend days. He really works at it and it shows." He added, "He is a kind, loving, generous and thoughtful friend. A first-rate human being."

Mr. Bryant observed that while none of those qualities have anything to do with being an artist, "It is nice when they are one and the same. Frequently, they ain't."

Some of Mr. Murphy's best known and most public work is a set of huge, brilliantly-colored murals he painted more than 31 years ago in the Katharine Cornell Memorial Theatre in Tisbury. Other paintings hang in private homes across the Vineyard and the country.

Speaking from his home off Middle Road following Sunday's opening, Mr. Murphy said the job of gathering the paintings was undertaken by his family and friends. "They wouldn't let me come in on that, and I'm damn glad they didn't," he said.

Asked why he had agreed to the idea of a retrospective, Mr. Murphy paused and said, "Why did I? Well, I didn't."

Initially he told his family that it was something that ought to happen "after I die." But when it became clear that they were anxious to do it for themselves and it would not involve any work on his part, he gave the go-ahead.

Mr. Murphy said the paintings on display represent only a small portion of the portraits he did over that time period. But he was adamant that people not be asked to ship paintings, some of them his favorites, given the vast amount of work required on both ends.

On Saturday morning Mr. Murphy saw the collection for the first time when he went to the gallery by himself to line up the paintings and decide which ones would go where.

"So many of them I hadn't seen for years and years; it was like seeing old friends again, some of them gone already, but it was a fascinating thing for me," he said.

On Sunday Mr. Murphy did not go into the gallery. "Didn't need to," he said.

Mr. Murphy said the question of whether he would attend the opening or not "came up." In the end, a letter from a friend convinced him he should go. The last time Mr. Murphy attended a gallery opening of his work was 52 years ago, his first opening.

"After I was there I said to Polly 'I am never going to do that again,' and I didn't." It was a decision rooted in the essential honesty and character of the artist.

"What are people going to say? There you are, you are standing around your own stuff, you are not dead certain that it is the best thing in the world, and what are they going to say? They can't say, 'Oh boy, that really stinks.' They are just trying to make you happy by what they say."

He said, "You have to be a different kind of a person entirely to want to be there and to hear what people have to say because guys who do that must believe what they hear. I don't."

Stanley Murphy, the celebrated and beloved artist whose work is uniquely emblematic of the Vineyard's landscape, history, and people, died July 23, 2003 at his home on Middle Road, West Tisbury. He was 81 years old.

A Search for Brook Trout
Brings Hidden Rewards

Fly fisherman Tim Sheran sees the potential in the Mill Pond mud
puddle, and wonders why others do not.
(October 2016)

TIM SHERAN OF Vineyard Haven is not an advocate in the strict
sense of the word. He is not the kind of guy who raises his voice
at a public meeting to exhort people to action. An expert fly fisherman, he knows what he knows, and if you ask, he will tell you what
he thinks.

Tim knows that Mill Pond in West Tisbury is a fake — an artificial
mud puddle created by a dam that chokes off the natural flow of native
brook trout and other species — and that the swans that grace its surface are an invasive species that are as harmful as the phragmites that
have supplanted native bulrushes around Island waterbodies.

And he knows that with some effort, the brook could be
restored to its natural beauty. Because he has seen it and fished it.

The Quashnet River in Falmouth and Red Brook in Wareham/
Plymouth offer two examples. Tim has fished both streams, and is
convinced that anyone who has any doubts about what Mill Brook
might look like with its dams removed needs only to visit either
place — preferably carrying a fly rod, but fishing skill is not a pre-
requisite to be able to appreciate their beauty, he said.

Tim Sheran holds a native
brook trout that took a fly.

Tim, 39, grew up in Western Massachusetts and visited the
Island with his family as a kid. His résumé includes professional
bicycle racer. He moved to the Island years ago, and used to
install tile for a living. Married and with a young son and a
new business, Cottage City Bicycle in Oak Bluffs, he still finds
time to fish. When I spoke to him on Sunday, he had just spent
the predawn hours casting for a big bluefish, and the morning
casting for albies in the driving wind and rain, without much
success.

Our conversation began months ago in the summer, when I
encountered him in the parking lot at Alley's. He was going trout
fishing, an unusual pursuit on an Island where the focus is on the
salt and the striped bass is king.

Tim told me that for years he has explored the small streams
and brooks of the Island in search of trout, which still survive in
scattered, hidden pools.

"I barely know the names of any of the water that I've fished here," he said. "Seeing a stream on the side of the road and just walking up it; that's how a lot of my fishing goes."

Tim acquired his passion and knowledge fishing for trout on a piece of the Willimantic River near his family's summer cottage. Although he is never far from a beach, he still rises to the call of trout.

"For me, hiking into the woods — getting away from people — it's just the adventure. Hiking down some stream, crawling through pricker bushes, sliding down embankments to catch that one little trout that you see sitting in that pool. That's kind of why I like to do it."

The reward is in the effort and the discovery. "I've never kept a brook trout, ever, on Martha's Vineyard," Tim said.

Mill Brook is not the only degraded stream in Massachusetts, but it may be the only one where the inhabitants resist the notion that a natural watercourse is superior to an artificial one, and twist themselves into knots coming up with environmental reasons to defend it. The Quashnet River and Red Brook provide prime examples of what can be accomplished when environmental science prevails over sentiment.

"It's an old cranberry bog that the Sea Run Brook Trout Coalition came in and rehabbed," Tim said. "That stream is one of the most amazing places; the amount of fish in there; the size of the fish in there; you are a mile and a half, two miles from the ocean, and there are 12-inch herring running up this three-foot-wide stream. And in the fall when the fry come down, my buddy hooked this 14-inch male brook trout — hooked jaw — it was pretty cool."

Tim said there is nothing that prevents Mill Brook, or any other brook on the Island, from being transformed. He said the nostalgia people feel for the pond is misplaced.

"Honestly, in a year it will rehab itself. It will still be beautiful … it will fix itself real quick. Of course, I want to see a trout stream over just seeing a stagnant puddle with invasive swans living in it."

Tim thinks it is not out of the question that in the future, he could catch sea run trout, known as salters, in Tisbury Great Pond. It is a dream he has.

The brook trout is a native New Englander. It is part of our heritage, and Mill Brook was once among the many prolific trout streams in southeastern Massachusetts.

In 1833, Dr. Jerome V.C. Smith, a medical doctor and author of "The Natural History of the Fish of Massachusetts," speaking of trout, described what he saw at Mill Brook: "In no place, however, do we remember to have seen them in such abundance as in Dukes County, upon Martha's Vineyard.... It was here in the month of November last, and of course in their spawning time; while returning home from a ramble among the heaths and hills of Chilmark and Tisbury, that crossing the principal brook of the island, our attention was attracted towards the agitated state of the water, and never do we recollect so fully to have realized the expression of its being 'alive with fish' as on this occasion."

It is the history and heritage of the brook trout, and its link to our fishing past, that captivates Tim, a member of the derby committee who spends plenty of time during the fall classic in pursuit of big fish. But the pleasure he gets from fishing is all relative, and has nothing to do with size.

"For me, getting a bite from a trout is more important than catching something that weighs 30 pounds," he said.

Epilogue

While compiling and winnowing columns for this book I realized that I have been writing stories about Martha's Vineyard for more than a quarter of a century. Over that span of time I have watched children grow to adulthood and become fathers and mothers, and I have mourned the loss of men and women who, to me, embodied the distinctive character of Martha's Vineyard Island. A number of the people identified in these columns — Walter Ashley, Fred Hehre, Jimmy Klingensmith, Bonito Ed, to name just a few — now fish or hunt only in spirit.

Although I do not feel old, it is inescapably true that since I first sat at a computer in the offices of The Martha's Vineyard Times, almost always on a Tuesday evening and up against a Wednesday afternoon deadline, my mustache, once brown, is now mostly white.

Frequently, when I began to write a fishing story I would not quite know where I would end up. But Islanders, on their own, tell a good story, and more often than not my role was to step out of the way. I did just that on the night I listened to my taped interview with Bob "Hawkeye" Jacobs, as he told me matter-of-factly about how he stripped down to his underwear and jumped off Memorial Wharf in Edgartown Harbor to try and free a false albacore after his fishing line caught up beneath the Pied Piper passenger ferry — an action utterly irrational to anyone but a derby fisherman — I knew I had struck column gold. All I had to do was let Hawkeye tell his tale.

Of course, not every column came so easily. There were nights when I sat quietly thinking about how best to tell a story. For the most part, I tried to think of writing a column as a conversation with friends, about other friends. That was how I approached the story of Albert "Angie" Angelone. Now, I seldom fish at Mink Meadows, where Angie was found lifeless on the beach, without thinking of this wonderful quirky guy who kept his background secret, and would, when he passed along a piece of fishing information in his unmistakable Jersey accent, always add, "Protect it wit your life."

When I began working at The Times we were a weekly. When I left in October 2016 we were essentially a daily — even an hourly. The increased emphasis on feeding the online news maw leaves me concerned that there will be less time for future columnists to devote to telling — really passing along — full, rich stories, or whether newspapers will even welcome columnists to write about fishing, deer hunting and waterfowling at all.

Thankfully, this Island community still appreciates its outdoor heritage. These stories recall the traditions and the people who have enriched Martha's Vineyard. A new generation follows in their footsteps.

87546374R00159

Made in the USA
Columbia, SC
21 January 2018